Be a $mart
Horse Buyer

A Guide To Avoiding Common Mistakes
And Finding The *Right* Horse For You

By Bob Avila

with Sue M. Copeland

Be a Smart Horse Buyer
Bob Avila, with Sue M. Copeland

Horse & Rider Magazine / Source Interlink Media, Gaithersburg, MD

First Published in 2007 by Horse & Rider Magazine / Source Interlink Media
Equine Network
656 Quince Orchard Road, #600
Gaithersburg, MD 20878
301-977-3900

VP, Group Publishing Director: Susan Harding
Director, Product Marketing: Julie Beaulieu
Editorial Director: Cathy Laws

Photographer: Cappy Jackson
Book Design: Lauryl Eddlemon Graphic Design
Cartoonist: Jim Paul, Sr.

Printed in the USA.

Order by calling 800-952-5813 or online at www.HorseBooksEtc.com

ISBN 13:978-1-929164-41-7

Library of Congress Cataloging-in-Publication Data

Avila, Bob.
  Be a smart horse buyer / Bob Avila, with Sue M Copeland.
    p. cm.
  ISBN 978-1-929164-41-7
  1. Horses. 2. Horses--Buying. I. Copeland, Sue M. II. Title.
  SF285.A95 2007
  636.1--dc22
                          2007043236

ABOUT THE AUTHORS

BOB AVILA   Born in 1951 in Half Moon Bay, California, the future world champion was the only child of Don Avila, a former rodeo cowboy turned professional trainer, and Pat Avila (now Pat Berry), an avid horsewoman.

Bob, who began showing as a child, says his mentors were trainers Don Dodge, Tony Amaral Sr., Harry Rose Sr., Clyde Kennedy, and Jimmy Williams. At the height of their careers during the 1950s and '60s, these legendary Californians, who themselves were influenced by the Vaquero methods, influenced bloodlines, tack, riding styles, and presentation in ways still apparent today.

"I realize how lucky I was to have had those great horsemen as direct influences so early in my life," Bob says. "I absorbed things from each one, starting at a very young age, that otherwise would have taken half a lifetime to learn."

Bob is now a mentor in his own right, teaching his insights and methods to young apprentices, many of whom have gone on to successful careers. Highlights of Bob's career include multiple American Quarter Horse Association world and reserve world championships in cutting, reining, working cow horse, Western riding, and halter, as well as three wins at the National Reined Cow Horse Snaffle Bit Futurity, and the prestigious open championship at the National Reining Horse Association Futurity.

In 1996, Bob was named the AQHA Professional Horseman of the Year, in honor of his many achievements in and contributions to the Quarter Horse industry. In June 2006, he took both All-Around Stock Horse Champion and reserve champion honors at the Magnificent 7 competition at the Western States Horse Expo, which features seven of the world's most skilled horsemen. In 2007, he earned a repeat win at the Magnificent 7 aboard Brother White, owned by Dana Mandela (Bob's wife). That same year, he won the World's Greatest Horseman title (his second) aboard Light N Fine, owned by Alan and Kay Needle.

His Avila Training Stables, Inc., is located in Temecula, California, where he lives with Dana (an avid horsewoman). To learn more about Bob's successful techniques, go to www.bobavila.net.

SUE M. COPELAND   An award-winning journalist in the equine field, Sue is a lifelong horse owner. She's the former editor of *Horse & Rider Magazine*, a Source Interlink Media publication. There she garnered numerous writing and editing awards, including the coveted American Horse Publication's General Excellence award for the magazine and its team. In the late '90s, she stepped back from the editorship to pursue book projects, writing, and consulting.

Sue is creator and editor of *Hands-On Horse Care*, which won the AHP's Best Equine-Related Book honor, and creator and co-author of its sister book, *Hands-On Senior Horse Care*. She is co-author, with Dr. John Hamil, of *Hands-On Dog Care*. That book was nominated for excellence by the Dog Writers Association of America, and won a Glyph award for Best Book from the Arizona Book Publishers Association.

Sue remains a consulting editor for *Horse & Rider*. She and her husband, Rick, share their Richmond, Texas, farm with their dogs and horses. Their Paint Horse gelding, CMF Distant Drums (shown above), earned the 2003 American Paint Horse Association World Championship title in junior working hunter with trainer Chuck Briggs in the irons. Sue also shows "Drummer" in hunter/jumper competition.

ACKNOWLEDGEMENTS

This book was quite an undertaking, and I have several people to thank because without them it wouldn't exist:

- First of all, Sue, you've been outstanding to work with; it's been a real pleasure to collaborate with someone who not only knows her job, but also understands the horse world so well.

- Dr. Kurt Heite, you are a true asset to this book, and to our lives and our horses as well (Preacher thanks you too!).

- Doug Carpenter, your friendship has meant a great deal to me, and I thank you for all of your knowledge and input in this project.

- Jim Paul Sr., you are one of a kind, and I am so honored to have your artwork and humor in this book.

- Tucker Allen, thank you for being a great kid!

- To my staff at the ranch, thanks for putting up with all of the photo shoots, and for jumping in a few shots when we needed you.

- Many thanks to Alan and Kay Needle for providing such a beautiful facility. It's a great place to come to work every day.

- Our thanks to Julie Beaulieu, Director of Product Marketing for Source Interlink Media's Equine Network, for your help in getting this book published.

- Hat's off to Cappy Jackson, our award-wining photographer and a lifelong horsewoman, whose beautiful photos help illustrate the points on these pages.

- To Lauryl Suire Eddlemon, Art Director, for pulling the text and photos together on these pages with talent, speed, and professionalism.

- And finally to my wife, Dana, thank you for all of the help, patience, love, and support. (And, for being our go-to model in this book.)

—*Bob Avila*

CONTENTS

Horse shopping can be so fun, yet so frustrating. You can save some of that frustration if you shop smart. That's what this book will help you do.

CHAPTER 1

Introduction
And General Tips

Buying a horse can be fun, exciting—and frustrating.
I know; I buy and sell horses as part of my living as a
trainer. And I've probably made almost every mistake I'll
talk about in this book. That's why I can help you.

Based on what I've learned, I'll show you how to avoid the most common horse-buying errors. I'll help you determine exactly what kind of horse you really need, then tell you how to find him (and approximately how much you'll pay). I'll also tell you how to get help from a pro when you shop (something I highly recommend), plus how to thoroughly evaluate any horse you try, from test-ride tips to a prepurchase exam.

In addition, I'll cover shopping on the Internet, buying your child's first horse, how to shop at a sale (and when not to), how to evaluate sale videos, and more. Along the way I'll talk about red flags that indicate you should walk away from a particular horse (or seller), and give you some insights into how to evaluate conformation and athletic ability.

As you'll learn, no horse is perfect, so I'll also share what vices and problems I can—and can't—live with.

Before we get into the details of smart horse buying, though, I'd like to share 10 global tips that'll help you avoid "Mr. Wrong" as you search for "Mr. Right."

1. Leave your emotions at the door. Emotions are a seller's dream. When you show them, he or she starts to see dollar signs. That's great for the seller, but dangerous for you.

So think with your head, not your heart, when you shop. It's your heart that can cause you to fall head over heels in love with an unbroke 2-year-old stallion when you really need a 10-year-old, super-broke gelding. Listening to your heart may be okay when you're shopping for shoes, or even a car. But when you end up with the wrong horse, you can get hurt.

2. Look past color. You may have a thing for bays or grays (always popular). Roans are "in" right now. I've had people call and say "My daughter *really* wants a palomino with two white socks…." That's putting the emphasis on a very incidental thing. And a bad horse with a good color is still a bad horse.

3. Be realistic about your abilities. If a horse you try seems like more horse than you can ride or handle, pass him up. If he's like that in a familiar setting, you can bet he'll turn into even more horse when you get him home, which will be unfamiliar to him. You'll find another one more suitable to your needs, believe me.

4. Be smart about gender. It's hard to go wrong with a good, quiet gelding. However, mares can make great horses, too. But some can be "mare-ish" during their heat cycles, meaning cranky, sore-sided, and distracted; that's a risk you take with a mare. Be sure to ask the seller about a mare's

A good horse is a good horse, regardless of color. And a bad horse with a good color is still a bad horse.

behavior when she's "in season." Stallions, in my opinion, are for professionals only. Even the best-minded stud will constantly test you. They also require special living arrangements to keep them, other horses, and you safe. They are dangerous in the wrong hands.

5. Take your time. You may be in a big hurry to buy your kid or yourself a horse. Or, you may be tired of looking and just ready to buy something. Just say "whoa," and take a deep breath. By taking your time to properly evaluate each prospect you look at, you'll best insure you end up with a horse that's appropriate for you. If you rush, you up the odds that you'll end up with one that's inappropriate. In other words, NO IMPULSE BUYS!

6. Avoid falling in love with a horse in the show or sales ring. All horses look their best in those situations. They're supposed to. But any flaw you observe there will be magnified when one steps outside that environment and you get him home. Arrange to see the horse in a natural setting, then use what you learn in this book to fully evaluate him.

7. Take notes. Keep a written record for each horse. See the "Smart Buyer Questionnaire" on page 92. Make copies of it and use them to keep track of horses you're interested in, and have looked at. That way, you'll know exactly what you liked—and didn't like—about a particular horse so you can make the best decision.

8. Take pictures. Consider, too, taking a digital camera or a video recorder with you when trying each horse, so you'll have a photographic or videographic record to which you can refer.

9. Avoid shopping in bad weather. That may sound funny, but I've found that weather can affect your decisions in a negative way. (It can also negatively impact how a horse behaves.) For instance, I once shopped in a snowstorm after having traveled a long way to look at a horse. I was so anxious to go get warm that I skipped some steps and bought the horse just so I could go home. Bad move. It wasn't a horse I would've bought under better circumstances. I've had friends say the same thing. If you have a choice, opt to wait for decent weather to shop.

10. Pretty is... I'm all about pretty horses. But too often I see people skip over a really good horse that's kind of plain, but has a great work ethic, in favor of a drop-dead-gorgeous one with a bad mind. That's a huge mistake. As my friend, professional agent Doug Carpenter, says, "I'd rather have a worker bee that's enthusiastic about his job than a queen bee that's a pain in the butt." I think that says it all. (See Doug's advice about buying at a sale on page 77.)

You'll find lots more tips like this on the pages of this book, ones I've learned (and earned) over years of buying and selling horses. Use them, then enjoy the shopping process. And, ultimately...your new horse.

Are you out to buy a world-caliber show horse? Or do you really need a horse you can enjoy on the trail or at local events? Knowing exactly what you need will help make your shopping experience easier.

CHAPTER 2

Meet Your Match

Does what you want in a horse really match what you need?
Use our checklist to find out. Plus, get a general idea of
what various levels of horses may cost.

2

Bob's Personal Experience

"I recently heard a middle-aged woman in less-than-ideal physical shape proudly talk about her new purchase. She'd bought a stud to show at halter. I mentally shook my head: That's not a good match.

Studs can be tough; they have a tendency to test you all the time and can hurt you if you're not careful. If she were to get in trouble with hers, I doubt she'd physically be able to get out of harm's way.

She wanted a stallion, though. Lots of people do. But sometimes what you want in a horse isn't what you need. That doesn't just apply to those of you with champagne taste on a beer budget. It's more about buying a horse that's *appropriate* for your plans and goals."

Appropriate: That's a word you'll be seeing a lot of in this book. For instance, maybe you've found that it's tough to find a nice, trained horse within your budget, but you can readily find lots of young, green horses. Be honest with yourself: Do you have the time, and more importantly the ability, to ride and train a youngster? If not, do you have the money for a trainer who can put the mileage on the horse he'll need in order to be safe—and appropriate—for you?

If your answer is "no" to those questions, a young and/or green horse is *inappropriate* for your needs. (For more information, see Chapter 6, "When Green Means No," page 45.)

Let's get back to your riding ability. It's been my experience that most riders overestimate their skills. An example: At every one of my Advanced Reining clinics, several people will show up who don't know what lead their horses are loping on. That's a basic skill most novice riders have mastered. Yet these folks obviously consider themselves "advanced" or they wouldn't be there.

To get an honest evaluation of your skills I suggest this: Pay a reputable trainer in your area to give you a lesson. Tell the trainer what you're looking for, horse-wise, and ask for an honest suitability assessment.

> I've just seen so many inappropriate buys made
> by amateurs who strike out on their own that
> I'm trying to prevent that from happening to you.

"Hey, Lady! You're the one who said you wanted a stud!"

This will be $50 or so well spent, believe me. In fact, I strongly recommend that you solicit a reputable trainer's or agent's help in finding an appropriate horse. That's not because I'm a trainer trying to feed business to my brethren. I've just seen so many inappropriate buys made by amateurs who strike out on their own that I'm trying to prevent that from happening to you.

This book will help prepare you to shop wisely, but a professional can look at a prospect in person and give you valuable feedback. For more information, see Chapter 3, "How (And Why) To Get Help From A Pro," page 19.

Matchmaker checklist

Finding the right horse to suit your needs can be tough. The first thing you need to do is decide what you'll want to do with him. To help you, we've put together this "Matchmaker Checklist." With it, we've outlined 11 common buying scenarios, what kind of horse would fit each one, and what such a horse might cost. (*Note:* These price ranges are rough estimates; prices can vary based on such factors as breed and region. For more information on breed and prices, see "The Breed Factor," page 17.)

Choose a scenario that best fits your desires to get an idea of what kind of horse (age, training, and attitude-wise) to shop for and how much you may need to spend. Then continue through the rest of the book to get the help you'll need for a smart buying experience.

Note: The horse in #1, below, will form the foundation for the horses in every category that follows. Think of it as a stripped-down car; you want the same safe, solid package at the core. The more bells and whistles (and power) you add, and the later the model, the more expensive the horse will be.

1. You desire: A companion horse.
Your goal is not to ride but rather to enjoy looking at, feeding, brushing, and caring for a horse. You may not have time to ride, or may no longer have the ability or desire. But you can provide a great home. (*Note:* This advice will also apply to a companion horse you plan to board, if you lack keep-at-home facilities.)

What you need: A mature, quiet, trustworthy gelding or mare that enjoys human attention.

What to shop for: A retired performance, trail, or therapeutic horse would be ideal. The horse should be "pasture sound" or better, meaning he's comfortable getting around his living area but may not be rideable. You may need to

A mature, quiet gelding can make an ideal companion horse. You can sometimes find a retired show horse that needs a good home (and might be free!).

For a companion horse you can ride lightly, look for the same horse as #1, but that is "serviceably sound" for light riding, per a veterinarian.

provide some extra care to maintain his comfort (which you'll have to be sure you can afford before you buy such a horse).

What you might pay: from $0 to around $5,000. That's right—some such horses are free to a good home. Show and performance barns often seek good homes at which to place horses that are no longer sound enough to work. Many therapeutic riding facilities do the same. Call facilities in your area to ask about such an opportunity. Be prepared to get checked out thoroughly as a placement home; if unknown to the horse owners/trainers/agents, they may ask for references and to visit your place.

2. A companion horse you can ride lightly.
You want a companion horse on which you (and/or your kids and grandkids) can occasionally mosey around your property.

What you need: Horse #1, but you'll need him to be "serviceably sound" for the amount of riding you'll do, as determined by a prepurchase veterinarian. (See Chapter 14: "The Prepurchase Exam," page 125.) The horse will need to be able to carry you comfortably on low-impact, low-mileage rides.

What to shop for: See #1, above.

What you might pay: $0 (see #1, above) to around $7,500.

3. A companion horse you can haul out with for long trail rides.

What you need: Everything outlined in #2, plus a horse that's sound and sane enough to carry you the distance you desire to ride.

What to shop for: Horse #2 that's been determined by a prepurchase exam to be serviceably sound for your level of trail riding. (Be sure, too, that he safely loads and hauls.)

What you might pay: $0 (see #1, above) to around $7,500.

When looking for a trail companion, opt for one that's sane and sound enough to carry you the distance safely.

4. All of the above, plus a horse you can haul to clinics and learn on.

You're an improvement-oriented person who wants to ride as often as possible, and learn as much as possible, so you can better yourself and your horse.

What you need: Horse #3, but with more "handle." By that I mean he has enough training that he's responsive to your requests to pick up all three gaits at a comfortable speed, and will easily turn and stop.

What to shop for: An older (aged 7 to 15), serviceably sound performance horse that's been hauled in the past would be ideal. Such a horse has already proven he's trainable, and will have enough handle to make your job easier. This is especially important if you have limited time due to family and job obligations.

What you might pay: From around $3,500 to $8,500.

If you want to haul to clinics, try to find a performance horse that's been hauled in the past, so you know he's trainable (and hauls!).

If you want to compete, buying a horse with some show mileage will ultimately save you time, money, and potential frustration.

5. All of the above, plus you'd also like to do a few local open or club shows on your own. In addition to clinics you'd like to test your skills in the show or performance arena, but lack the budget or desire for a trainer.

What you need: Horse #4, with these additions—he knows his leads, and has surefire steering and brakes. (If he doesn't guide and stop well, you'll be a hazard to others and to yourself at shows.)

What to shop for: See #4, with this addition—the horse has been competed on in the past. Buying a horse with some show mileage will save you the time, money, and effort it takes to get him acclimated to a show environment, which can be stressful to all involved.

What you might pay: Around $10,000 or under.

6. A horse you can keep at home and show competitively at a local level without regular professional help. First of all, you have to ask yourself: Do I have time to do it myself? You'll need that and dedication in order to be competitive.

What you need: Horse #5 with these additions—he's currently showing in (or has shown in) the

For do-it-yourselfers, a horse with some professional training and experience in your chosen event will help you be competitive, and will make both of your jobs easier.

event or events at which you plan to compete. You'll also need the time to haul to clinics whenever possible as a tune-up and to advance your horse's and your own skills.

What to shop for: A horse between the ages of 5 and 15 that's had some professional training. This horse should be competent and confident in your chosen event or you both might be set up for failure.

What you might pay: From around $7,500 to around $35,000. (Yes, that's right—$35,000. Some local shows in some areas are extremely competitive. The top figure in this and the rest of the show-horse matches reflects what you might pay for a horse you can consistently win on in such an area. You'll pay less for a horse that may be in the ribbons, but isn't a consistent winner.)

7. To have a **do-it-yourself show horse** you can take lessons on once or twice a week, to ratchet up your competitive edge. You're very improvement oriented and have the time and money to haul and show on a regular basis. You plan to compete regularly throughout the year.

What you need: A horse that's trained enough to stay tuned up for the show ring with minimal professional help. *You* need the ability to attend advanced clinics and to watch videos, and to extrapolate techniques from them you can use to improve both your and your horse's performances.

What to shop for: See #6. In addition, your horse will need the eye appeal, athletic ability, and experience to catch a judge's eye in subjectively judged events, or the talent to be competitive at your chosen level in speed events or any other competitive event.

What you might pay: From around $7,500 to around $35,000 (see #6, above).

Opting to do a lot of your own work with a show horse will require that you have the time and ability to haul out to lessons and clinics, plus watch videos, then take what you learn back home and apply it to your horse.

Shopping for a horse that you plan to keep in full training should include help from the trainer you'll be sending the horse to. You want him or her invested in the horse, to guarantee the best outcome for all involved.

8. To find a horse and keep him in full training.

You lack the time and/or facility to keep him at home, and want him ready to go (and safe) when you *can* ride (or show). You're striving to constantly improve your riding and your horse's performance, be it for the fun of it, or for the show ring.

What you need: Your trainer's help. If you're going to keep the horse in full training with him or her, he or she needs to like the horse, and be invested in his (and your) future. Having him or her be part of the shopping process helps make that happen. Trust me, that'll make everyone involved (including the horse) happier.

I can't tell you how many times I've had people go buy a horse on their own, then want to bring it to me for training. Nine times out of 10 it's not a horse I'd have picked to work with, or for that particular person. I'm at the point now that I can turn down horses I don't want to work with. But some trainers don't have that luxury. Sure, most will do their best for the horse, but you'll maximize your training dollars (and your success) if you include your trainer on the front end.

What to shop for: Since you'll have a trainer's help in choosing and working with the horse, you may be able to get a younger, greener horse. This is particularly true if you're not in a hurry, and have the budget to pay indefinitely for full-time training. However, if you want to ride *now* and can't afford full-time training for the long term, opt for a horse that your trainer thinks is appropriate for your current goals and riding ability.

What you might pay: From about $15,000 to $50,000 (again, this is for a horse that can consistently win at your level).

Even when you shop for a national-level horse with your trainer, your involvement will be key. After all, you're the one writing the check!

9. To train full-time—and show—with a national-level trainer.

You want to show at a national level and be competitive. You have the time and money to do it. You're looking for a positive, supportive relationship with the trainer and a chance to socialize at the barn and shows with the people you meet.

What you need: A reputable trainer who specializes in your chosen event. (If you haven't yet picked a specific event, attend some shows and study different classes to get a handle on what appeals to you.) For how to find a good trainer, see Chapter 3, "How (And Why) To Get Help From A Pro," page 19.

What to shop for: At this level you'll most likely work with your trainer to find a horse that suits your ability and is competitive at a national level. That said, you should be involved in the process. The ultimate choice will be yours—you're the one writing the check.

What you might pay: From about $35,000 to about $75,000.

If you aspire to the top-tier of your sport, your trainer's help in choosing a suitable horse will be critical. If you don't trust him or her enough to find you a horse, you need a new trainer.

10. To be a **world-class competitor**.

You've got the goal of reaching—and winning at—the top tier of your event. You're extremely competitive. You have a relationship (or will establish one) with a trainer who can help you meet your goal.

What you need: Lots of dedication and talent. You'll need time and money, too, but it's been my experience the first two requirements are the most important. Dedication and talent can open a lot of doors.

What to shop for: At this level about 95 percent of the horse-selection process will be left to your trainer. If you don't trust him or her to play that large a role in your horse-buying journey, you need a new trainer.

What you might pay: From around $40,000 and up (you can go into the six figures).

11. To be an "investment" buyer.

You hope to "buy low and sell high." You see any horse you purchase as a way to make some money.

What you need: A reality check. Horses aren't cars, gold, or pork bellies. There is no "Kelley Blue Book" for assessing value. Plus, they get sick, lame, and can die. Buying and selling horses is risky business.

What to shop for: A horse you wouldn't mind keeping for the rest of his life. That's essential for two reasons: 1) Something could happen to him and you could get stuck with him for the rest of his life; and 2) If you like the horse that much, chances are other people will, too. That means he's saleable.

A personal note: The advice I just gave you is my cardinal rule for buying investment horses. That's because every time I break my own rule, say by buying a horse I don't absolutely love and could easily keep for myself, I get burned when it comes time to sell him. Save yourself some pain and money—live by that rule.

If you want your resale market to be as broad as possible, pick one of the above categories, depending on your budget, and buy a horse that fits it. If the horse isn't quiet, safe, sane, and serviceably sound, good luck selling him.

What you might pay: See the individual categories outlined above.

To find an investment horse, shop for one that fits one of the categories outlined in this chapter. Then be sure you like him enough to keep him forever. Something could happen that makes that a reality (such as an injury). Plus, if you like him that much, chances are a buyer will.

The breed factor

In the Western horse industry, breed can make a difference in price. For instance, Quarter Horses tend to be at the top of the price category, especially when it comes to show horses.

You can generally buy "more horse" for your dollar if you opt for a similarly experienced Paint. Appaloosas of similar experience may be even less expensive. A true bargain can be Solid Paint Breds (SPBs), which are Paints that are born without enough color to qualify for the regular registry. While the American Paint Horse Association has added some classes at shows for SPBs, at this point they're not allowed to show against Paints with color at APHA events, which can lower their value.

If you compete in such non-APHA events as hunter/jumper, eventing, reining, or cutting, you can show an SPB. So if that's your competition of choice, or you're simply looking for a good trail horse, SPBs can be a very good deal.

With Arabians, prices can vary. While top-level show horses can be very expensive, an Arabian trail or low-level show horse may cost less than his Quarter Horse counterpart.

Since breed registration papers aren't necessary to compete in United States Hunter Jumper Association events (or in combined training/eventing and dressage), performance or performance potential tends to drive price more than breeding. Generally, national-level hunters, jumpers, and dressage horses are Warmbloods and can cost more than national-level horses in Western events. But of course, there are no rules when it comes to equine pricing, and there are always exceptions!

An agent will accompany you when you look at a horse, and offer an honest assessment about whether the horse is or isn't the right one for you.

CHAPTER 3

How (And Why) To Get Help From A Pro

Learn why hiring a trainer or agent to help with your horse hunt can be the smartest money you'll spend. (Plus, how to find a good one.)

3

"I once tried to save money by building my own hot rod, rather than hiring a pro to help me find one that was ready to go. The result? I ended up struggling for 3 years to build it, and spending twice the amount of money it would've cost me to buy a ready-made one. I also lost a ton of money when I sold the car.

Why the hot rod anecdote? Because I often see people try to do the same thing with horses. Rather than hiring a professional to help them find a horse appropriate to their goals and abilities, they strike out on their own. And often have results similar to mine with the do-it-yourself hot rod. They spend years and excess dollars trying to get the horse to a point at which they can enjoy him. (If they can ever get him to that point.)

Working with a pro doesn't take away from your horse-shopping experience. You still need to determine exactly what you want (which a pro can help you with), and to be a big part of the selection and test-ride process. In fact, working with a good pro can enhance the experience—and help make for a successful outcome."

I'm always surprised at how impulsive people are when it comes to buying horses. The same guy or gal that'll research a new car buy through *Consumer Reports* and the Internet, then drill the salesmen with questions will melt at the first horse he or she tries, and buy it.

I've never understood that mentality. If I were a layman looking to buy a horse, I'd go talk to people who know exactly how and where to find what I want and need. In fact, I just bought myself a hot rod car...but not before I enlisted expert help in doing so.

So how do you find good help? You hire someone who's an expert in the breed and/or activity you choose to do. Typically, this would be a trainer or agent who specializes in finding and selling horses. Here are some agent/trainer fast-facts:

Where to find one:

■ **Breed associations:** If you want a Paint, start with the American Paint Horse Association (APHA). If you want a Quarter Horse, go to the American Quarter Horse Association (AQHA). Same with a Tennessee Walker or Missouri Fox Trotter, or an Arabian. (For how to contact those associations and more, see "Association Resource Guide," page 25.)

Breed associations generally have Professional Horseman's or trainer/breeder lists. For instance, the AQHA can help recommend someone in your state and chosen event.

■ **Shows/events.** Go to an event or show that features your chosen activity. For instance, if you want a trail horse, go to an organized trail ride in your area and ask around. Tell people that you're looking for a reputable pro who can help you buy a good horse. Don't ask just one person; ask as many as you can. Keep track of the folks who get consistent thumbs up: They're the ones you want to talk to. If you hear consistently about people to avoid, pay attention. Then "vet" the names with the breed association, farriers, veterinarians, and other trainers in your area.

*"Like my new horse? I found him myself.
Now if I could only ride him . . . ."*

What you'll pay:

There are two typical approaches:

1. A flat percentage. Agents or trainers typically charge a percentage of a horse's sale price for their services (known as a "commission"), which generally is about 10%, although it could be slightly more, or slightly less. For a $10,000 horse, that would be around $1,000.

(continued on page 22)

Before you hire an agent ...

Get serious. Hire an agent only when you're serious about buying. If you just want to "tire kick," you'll waste his or her time—and earn resentment.

Narrow down your criteria. Have a reasonable idea of what you're looking for, based on the criteria in Chapter 2, "Meet Your Match." An agent *can* help you decide what you want, but he or she will need educated input from you in order to be able to offer advice.

Establish a budget. Know exactly what your top dollar will be for a horse, adding any potential commission or looking fees. It's unfair to an agent (and to sellers) for you to look at horses you can't afford.

"Vet" the agent. I'm gonna say it again: Before you hire anyone to help you find a horse, be sure to ask for references, and check his or her reputation with breed associations, barns, veterinarians, farriers, tack and feed stores, and shows/events the person is associated with.

Find someone you trust—then listen to him or her. Determine, before you hire, if this is a person you respect and trust. At events, stand back and watch how he or she treats horses, clients, and staff. If it's with care and respect, that's a good thing. If it's not, that's a bad thing. I'll even go check out a person's rig. It doesn't have to be fancy, but if it's clean and in good repair, that's generally a good sign that the rest of the business will be, too. If not, trust your gut and keep looking. When you finally find someone with whom you click, listen to his or her advice. After all, that's what you're paying for.

To check out a potential trainer/agent, attend an event and observe how he or she treats clients, horses, and staff. If it's with care and respect, that's a good thing.

I recommend you check out his or her rig, too. If it's well cared for, chances are his business will be, too.

When you finally find someone with whom you click, listen to his or her advice. After all, that's what you're paying for.

Negotiate (and get in writing) your agreed-upon fee *before* you hire an agent. Several other items to discuss with your agent:

Will there be expenses? Ask the pro if he or she expects to incur any expenses above and beyond the agreed-upon commission. If so, get an estimate in writing. *(Note:* If I find someone a horse at a show or event I'm already attending, I don't charge expenses. But if I make a special trip to look at a specific horse, I might—with the prospective buyer's permission.)

The seller may pay the commission. You may not owe a commission if the seller pays it. In fact, the seller often prices a horse to include a commission, or "finder's fee," to whomever connects him to a buyer. In sales in which I'm involved, this is typical. The buyer pays an agent's expenses (if there are any); the seller pays the commission/finder's fee. (And if another pro linked me to the horse, I'll split the finder's fee/commission with him or her.) However, this can vary from sale to sale.

There should be only one commission paid. Disreputable people may try to "double-dip," meaning they'll try to get a full commission from the buyer *and* the seller. That's why it's important to "vet" an agent before you hire one, as mentioned under "Where To Find One," page 20. However, you can always ask the seller if he or she will be paying the commission, should you decide to buy a horse.

2. Per horse looked at. You may be able to hire some agents on a "piecemeal" basis. By that, I mean you may be able to hire them specifically to accompany you when you go try a horse you've found. Plan to pay $50 or less per "look," plus expenses such as meals and mileage, if accrued. Again, get any fees and anticipated expenses in writing *before* you start shopping. If such an agent ends up finding you a horse and gets a commission from the seller, he or she may deduct fees and expenses from that.

Services to expect:

■ **When paying a flat percentage (commission).**

> *Find prospective horses.* He or she will seek out
> and screen horses for you to look at, based on the
> criteria you've discussed with him or her. (See
> "Before You Hire An Agent…" page 21.) Depending
> on the horse, this could include pedigree research,
> checking performance records, talking to trainers,
> veterinarians, and farriers who know the horse, and
> other such "background checks."

> *Schedule appointments.* The agent will arrange for
> you to go see horses that seem suitable.

Opposite Page: Your agent will find you horses to look at,
research those horses, and set up appointments for you to try
them. **Top:** He (or she) will then accompany you if you opt to go
see the horse, and help evaluate whether the horse is suitable to
your needs. **Above:** He'll then share his thoughts with you.
Listen to them. You hired him for his expertise.

Above: **The agent will then negotiate terms of the sale...** ***Above right:*** **...and work with you to close the deal, if the horse passes a prepurchase exam (which the agent will also arrange).**

I've seen agents save buyers major headaches,
and find them perfect matches. And I've seen buyers
that haven't used agents make major mistakes.

Accompany you. He or she will go with you to help evaluate a prospective horse and will take an active role in verifying suitability through questions to the seller, handling, and riding the horse (if applicable).

Offer an honest assessment. After you've both evaluated a prospect, the agent will offer his or her opinion as to whether this could be—or isn't—the right horse for you.

Negotiate terms of sale. If you decide to buy a horse, the agent will negotiate the terms of sale. Not only will this include price, but it could also include breeding contracts for sales that include breeding stock.

Handle the prepurchase exam. If you agree with the seller on terms of a sale, the agent will then arrange to have a prepurchase exam performed. (See Chapter 14, "The Prepurchase Exam," page 125.) The agent will discuss the veterinarian's findings with him or her, then relay them to you, helping you to interpret whether any findings could negate the sales terms.

Close the deal. If the sale is a "go," based on prepurchase exam findings, the agent will work with you and the seller to close the deal. He or she can also help arrange transportation, if necessary, to get the horse to your facility.

- **Per horse looked at.**

    Accompany you. He or she will go with you to help evaluate a prospective horse and will take an active role in verifying suitability through questions to the seller, handling, and riding the horse (if applicable).

    Offer an honest assessment. After you've both evaluated a prospect, the agent will offer his or her opinion as to whether this could be—or isn't—the right horse for you.

As you can see, a commissioned agent can be a true asset in your horse hunt. I highly recommend you use one, and I don't just say that because I make part of my living buying and selling horses. I say it because I've seen agents save buyers major headaches, and find them perfect matches. And I've seen buyers that haven't used agents make major mistakes.

Association resource guide

Your guide to contact info for major breed and show associations

Below is a list of major breed and show associations; please note that contact information is subject to change. Due to space constraints, it doesn't include all such associations.

American Miniature Horse Association
5601 S. Interstate 35W
Alvarado, TX 76009
Ph: 817-783-5600
Fax: 817-783-6403
Email: Information@amha.org
www.amha.org

American Paint Horse Association
P. O. Box 961023
Fort Worth, TX 76161-0023
Ph: 817-834-2742
Fax: 817-834-3152
Email: askapha@apha.com
www.apha.com

American Shetland Pony Club and American Miniature Horse Registry
81 B Queenwood Road
Morton, IL 61550
Ph: 309-263-4044 Fax: 309-263-5113
Email: info@shetlandminiature.com
www.shetlandminiature.com

American Morgan Horse Association
122 Bostwick Road
Shelburne, VT 05482
Ph: 802-985-4944
Fax: 802-985-8897
Email: info@morganhorse.com
www.morganhorse.com

American Quarter Horse Association
1600 Quarter Horse Drive
Amarillo, TX 79104
Ph: 806-376-4811
Fax: 806-349-6403
Email: jhancock@aqha.org
www.aqha.com

American Warmblood Society
2 Buffalo Run Road
Center Ridge, AR 72027
Ph: 501-893-2777
Fax: 501-893-2779
Email: aws@americanwarmblood.org
www.americanwarmblood.org

(continued)

Association resource guide (continued)

Appaloosa Horse Club
2720 W. Pullman Road
Moscow, ID 83843
Ph: 208-882-5578 Fax: 208-882-8150
Email: marketing@appaloosa.com
www.appaloosa.com

Arabian Horse Association
10805 E. Bethany Drive
Aurora, CO 80014
Ph: 303-696-4500 Fax: 303-696-4599
Email: info@arabianhorses.org
www.arabianhorses.org

**Friesian Horse Association of
North America**
4037 Iron Works Parkway, Suite 160
Lexington, KY 40511-8483
Ph: 859-455-7430 Fax: 859-455-7457
Email: tjensen@fhana.com
www.fhana.com

**International Andalusian and
Lusitano Horse Association**
101 Carnoustie N, #200
Birmingham, AL 35242
Ph: 205-995-8900 Fax: 205-995-8966
Email: office@ialha.org
www.ialha.org

**Jockey Club (Thoroughbreds)
Executive Offices:**
40 E. 52nd Street
New York, NY 10022
Ph: 212-371-5970 Fax: 212-371-6123
www.jockeyclub.com
Registry:
821 Corporate Drive
Lexington, KY 40503-2794
Ph: 859-224-2700 Fax: 859-224-2710
www.jockeyclub.com

**Missouri Fox Trotting Horse Breed
Association**
P.O. Box 1027
Ava, MO 65608
Ph: 417-683-2468
www.mfthba.com

National Reining Horse Association
3000 NW 10th Street
Oklahoma City, OK 73107
Ph: 405-946-7400 Fax: 405-946-8425
www.nrha.com

**National Reined Cow Horse
Association**
13181 US Hwy 177
Byars, OK 74831
Ph: 580-759-4949 Fax: 580-759-3999
Email: nrcha@nrcha.com
www.nrcha.com

National Walking Horse Association
4059 Iron Works Parkway #4
Lexington, KY 40511
Ph: 859-252-6942 Fax: 859-252-0640
www.nwha.com

**North American Peruvian Horse
Association**
3095 Burleson Retta Road
Burleson, TX 76028
Ph: 707-447-7574 Fax: 707-447-2450
www.napha.net

Norwegian Fjord Horse Registry
1203 Appian Drive
Webster, NY 14580
Ph: 585-872-4114
Fax: 585-787-0497
Email: registrar@nfhr.com
www.nfhr.com

Palomino Horse Association
Route 1, Box 125
Nelson, MO 65347
Ph: 660-859-2064
www.palominohorseassoc.com

Palomino Horse Breeders of America
15253 E. Skelly Drive
Tulsa, OK 74116-2637
Ph: 918-438-1234
Fax: 918-438-1232
www.palominohba.com

Pinto Horse Association of America
7330 NW 23rd Street
Bethany, OK 73008
Ph: 405-491-0111
Fax: 405-787-0773
www.pinto.org

**Tennessee Walking Horse Breeders'
& Exhibitors' Association**
P.O. Box 286
250 N. Ellington Parkway
Lewisburg, TN 37091
Ph: 931-359-1574
www.twhbea.com

United States Equestrian Federation
4047 Iron Works Parkway
Lexington, KY 40511
Ph: 859-258-2472
Fax: 859-231-6662
www.usef.org

*If you're looking for an
association not listed here,
Google it on the Internet.*

Buying a young horse for your child "to grow up with" is like hiring a little kid to tutor your little kid—except that a young horse could physically hurt your child.

CHAPTER 4

Five Buying Myths Busted

Learn why common misconceptions can lead you down the path to the wrong horse.

"Years ago I had a guy bring me a 2-year-old gelding he'd bought for his 14-year-old daughter. This wasn't a good-quality horse, but even if it had been, his concept of his daughter "growing up" with the horse was a wrong one. This girl was eager to ride and show; she only had a few years in the youth ranks left.

I immediately told the father that the horse was inappropriate for his daughter's age, experience, and goals. I pointed out that by the time he'd be mature and seasoned enough for her to show, she'd likely be aged out of the youth division. Her father, however, didn't want to hear it. As a result, his poor kid grew increasingly frustrated. She had a horse that wasn't broke enough for her to ride or show.

I did what I could for them, but 2-year-olds take time and patience. As often happens when stuck with an inappropriate horse, the girl ultimately lost interest. She never did get to show. She fell victim to her father's steadfast belief in one of the oldest myths in horse buying. See "Myth #1" on the following page."

Myth #1: "You can grow up and/or learn together."

■ **What it is:** People tell me constantly that they want to buy a young horse for little Johnny or Janie, so horse and child can "grow up together." Even naïve grownups shopping for their own horses will look at young ones, thinking "we can learn together." Wrong!

■ **Why it's wrong:** Buying a young horse for your child is like hiring a 5-year-old kid to tutor *your* 5-year-old kid. The big difference? A horse, especially a young, inexperienced one, can hurt (or worse) your child. Horses aren't puppies.

You always want your kid to learn from an older, seasoned adult. Why wouldn't you look for the same thing in a horse? Ditto if you're an adult looking to learn a new sport. You don't turn to a fellow rookie for how-to advice. You seek knowledge from someone who's trustworthy and who's been doing it longer than you have, so you can learn. You should look for the same when shopping for a horse.

■ **How to avoid it:** When shopping for a kid's horse, or a horse you can learn on (not with), look for a seasoned schoolmaster with some good mileage that's respectful and currently employed in the very job you'll want him to do.

■ **Final word:** Kids are only kids for so long (same with grown-up kids who feel an age-related deadline). If you have to spend years training a young or green horse, you may lose that enjoyment time. Why not get something you can enjoy right away?

Plus, I've seen too many kids and novice adults scared and/or discouraged by horses that are too young and green. You may spend less on the front end for such a horse than you would on a broke, seasoned one, but you'll pay for it in the long haul in training dollars and potential fear and frustration.

Too many kids and novices get scared or discouraged by horses that are too young or green. That's why I recommend you buy a broke one.

If someone tries to tell you that you "can make money on this one," watch out. Who can guarantee something like that? I buy and sell horses for a living, and I sure can't!

Myth #2: "You can make money on this one."

- **What it is:** The seller, your friends, or your family tell you that you can make money on a certain horse, by buying and re-selling him for a profit.

- **Why it's wrong:** I don't think any true horseman can honestly tell you you'll make money on a horse. I know I wouldn't. (The closest I'll come is saying, "You have a *chance* of making money on this one.")

  Buying and selling horses is risky. They get sick. They break. Like boats and recreational vehicles, they can depreciate with age and mileage. The economy can change. Any number of things can happen that can make any hope of a profit (or breaking even) evaporate like morning dew.

- **How to avoid it:** If things look too good to be true, they usually are. It generally takes a professional eye and contacts to make money with horses, and even then you can lose. (I know I have!) In my experience, it's a gamble. I'd say only about 10 percent of people who try to profit from buying and selling horses actually do.

  Before you decide to buy to sell, ask yourself whether you want your horses to be a hobby or a business. You can't usually mix the two, at least successfully. If you go the hobby route, don't take the fun out of horses by trying to make money with them.

- **Final word:** If you want to buy an "investment" horse, find yourself a reputable agent (see Chapter 3 for how to find one), and state your goal from Day 1. Even then, be prepared to lose. It happens to the best of us.

Amateurs: Steer clear of stallions, regardless of how good minded a seller says one is. They will constantly test you, as this stud is doing. Horses are supposed to be fun. Buy a gelding!

To me, amateurs and stallions don't mix, period.

Myth #3: "This stud is just like a gelding."

- **What it is:** A sales pitch to get you to buy a stallion.

- **Why it's wrong:** To me, amateurs and stallions don't mix, period. Stallions test you all the time; it's their nature. That's how they survive in the wild, by being dominant. You have to watch them at all times, no matter how good minded they are.

- **How to avoid it:** Buy a gelding. I make my living dealing with horses, and geldings consistently make the best mounts and/or companions. They're not tormented by hormones like stallions (and mares) can be. A good gelding is a great bet.

No horse is "totally bombproof." Every horse will spook as this horse is, given the right (or wrong!) circumstances. Be suspect if a seller insists otherwise.

All horses can spook (and bite or kick). Anyone who tells you otherwise is suspect.

Myth #4: "He's totally bombproof."

■ **What it is:** A sales pitch from the seller, trying to tell you the horse is quiet and doesn't spook.

■ **Why it's wrong:** It's like saying, "My dog would never bite." (Or, "My horse would never kick or bite.") All dogs will bite under the right (or wrong!) circumstances. All horses can spook (and bite or kick). Anyone who tells you otherwise is suspect.

■ **How to avoid it:** Ask questions, lots of them. For instance, ask what the horse has been exposed to. Ask if he's ever spooked, and when or why. Press the point, if need be. It's okay to be skeptical, and the only dumb question is the one you're afraid to ask. If you like the horse, go to Chapter 12, and see if he passes the Test Ride.

■ **Final word:** When you try any horse, be sure to expose him to stimuli he'll likely encounter if you buy him. For a show horse, that would mean observing the horse at a horse show. For a trail horse, it would mean a test ride down a trail. If you have kids, watch how the horse reacts when children are at play. Exposing the horse to such situations *before* you buy him could save you frustration down the road.

Myth #5: "He's perfect for the job."

- **What it is:** A typical sales pitch used to try to sell you a horse that's *not* perfect for the job.

- **Why it's wrong:** Say for example you're looking at a halter-bred horse to use for reining, or an ex-racehorse to ride on the trails. Both would be as wrong as using a Tennessee Walking Horse to try to win a top barrel racing futurity. Such a horse isn't bred to do the job you're asking him to do. Sure, there are exceptions to every rule, and he'll try if he's good minded. But he'd have a much easier time (and you'll both be much happier) if he's doing the job he's bred to do.

I commonly see people stand stallions that are halter bred, breed them to cutting-horse mares, then sell the babies as reiners and working cow horses. Those foals aren't bred or built to rein or work cattle. I mean, you wouldn't buy a Volkswagen Bug to do a quarter-mile drag race, would you?

Go for suitability. Pick breeding that's *suitable* to your event. If you want to ride a Western pleasure horse, choose a horse that's bred top and bottom (sire and dam) for that event. If you want to trail ride, choose a breed (and mind) that's quiet and comfortable to ride. Same with reining, cutting, halter, or any specialized event. It's not fair to the horse or you if he can't easily do as you ask.

- **How to avoid it:** When you go horse shopping, find someone you trust in the event or activity of your choice, so you can find a horse suitable to your needs. I've had people come to my barn looking for a reiner, but accompanied by a dressage trainer. That trainer has no idea what a good reiner should look like, or do. Again, this is where a good, reputable agent will come in handy. He or she will know the bloodlines suited to your needs. The fee you'll pay for his or her services will be well worth the expertise you get in return. Save yourself (and your future horse) some heartache. See Chapter 3: "How (And Why) To Get Help From A Pro," page 19.

"Seriously, this 2-year-old Walking Horse will be perfect for your little Sally's barrel racing prospect."

Use the Internet for what it is: A valuable tool for locating prospects. But cyber-buyer, beware—avoid buying a horse sight unseen.

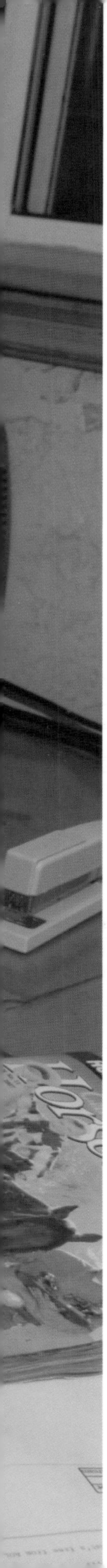

CHAPTER 5

The Pros—And Pitfalls—
Of Buying Off The 'Net

**The Internet can be a terrific resource for finding horses.
But it's truly cyber-buyer beware ...**

5

"Shopping for a horse on the Internet is like shopping for a home on the 'net. It's a great tool for finding prospects, but you darn sure don't want to buy one you haven't seen in person.

Yet I often hear of people who've bought horses sight unseen over the Internet. And I never hear of that working out. In fact, those folks usually end up coming to a professional like me to help them unload the horse because it didn't work.

I wouldn't buy anything over the Internet without having seen it first. That's especially true with horses. Doing so is asking for a disaster."

Bob's Personal Experience

You've heard about people who've used Internet matchmaking services to meet men or women. You probably have a girlfriend or relative who's done it. Chances are, she has a story like this: A guy who sells himself as tall, athletic, and good-looking in his photo and description turns out to be short, bald, and paunchy when she meets him in person. He either used an old photo or Photoshop to make himself look better. Hey, anything to make the "sale," right?

That's exactly what can happen when you shop for horses on the 'net. You can input your dream horse into the site's search engine: 15.2-hand gray gelding, 9 years old, bombproof, with a special favored bloodline, within XX miles of your home. And you'll probably find multiple horses that match, at least on the surface. But what lurks beneath the photo and "sell" copy is the million-dollar question.

That's why I'm extremely cautious about advising anyone to use the Internet for buying horses unless they follow my specific "Do's" and "Don'ts." If you're one of the legions of Internet shoppers looking for Mr. or Ms. Right, here's my advice:

DON'T buy a horse off the Internet sight unseen. Buying "blind" from any source (classified ads, etc.) carries a huge risk of you getting burned…and stuck with a horse that's not suitable for you (and that you may not be able to sell).

I've heard of all sorts of problems from buys like this, such as health and/or behavior trouble (see "Example of a 'Don't,'" opposite page). Yet, people still do it. Buying horses on the 'net isn't like buying collectibles on Ebay. A horse can show up with issues. Big issues.

My only exception to the "blind" rule would be if you know the horse's history, and the seller, very well (for instance, you've followed the horse's career, and have successfully bought horses through this agent before). Even then, you should look at a current video, thoroughly research the horse's current state of health and training (things change), and invest in a prepurchase exam performed by the veterinarian of your choice (see Chapter 14). Still, I think you're better off seeing what you get in person.

Don't use the Internet to shop? You can apply many of the tips in this chapter to shopping via "hardcopy" classified ads.

Example of a "DON'T"

A gal we know, an amateur who considered herself a savvy shopper, saw what appeared to be a terrific find on the Internet. The horse was pretty, athletic, and affordable—just what she wanted for a show prospect that she hoped to resell for a profit. He was located so far away from her, though, that she opted not to spend the time or money to go see him in person. After much back-and-forth with the seller, and looking at a video of the horse, the gal had the horse vetted and bought him.

When he arrived she was thrilled…until she rode him. Sure enough the horse was athletic: Every time she tried to ride him into an arena he turned into a bronc. He'd rear, buck, and turn himself inside out, anything to avoid going through the gate. He was dangerous. That's not a good trait in any horse, much less one you want to show (and sell). Needless to say, this little quirk was something the seller neglected to mention.

With nearly a year of intensive help from a trainer (something she hadn't budgeted for), and with the trainer acting as agent, the gal was finally able to sell the horse. She did *not* make a profit. But she did learn an expensive lesson. She now involves her trainer in horse buys, and ponies up the time and money it takes to go see a horse before making any buying decisions.

I'm extremely cautious about advising anyone to use the Internet for buying horses unless they follow my specific "Do's" and "Don'ts."

DO use the Internet for what it is: a valuable resource for finding prospects. Then do the following:

- **Call the seller/agent (or have your agent call him or her).** Use the "Buyer's Questionnaire" in Chapter 11 as a guide for finding out as much as you can about the horse's suitability for you. Be specific about what you're looking for. Think beyond your riding goals. For instance, if you'll be keeping the horse at home, ask about any vices, quirks, or issues that could make him unsafe to have around you or (perhaps novice) family members, and other horses, if you have them.

Example of a "DO"

My co-author, Sue Copeland, was looking for a hunter prospect. She spied a late 2-year-old Paint gelding for sale on one Internet site. The horse was being shown in Western pleasure futurities, winning money even though he was quickly "outgrowing" the event, size-wise (he was over 16.1 hands).

His description on the site told Sue several key things: He'd been hauled regularly; he had show mileage; and he was quiet and pretty enough for the pleasure ring, which meant he'd likely be quiet and pretty enough for a new career as a hunter.

First she sent an email asking very specific questions about temperament, health, size, training, and show record. She also described exactly what she was looking for: A Paint hunter prospect she could keep at home, haul to a trainer's for occasional lessons, and show in American Paint Horse Association competition. The horse, she specified, had to be quiet, sane, amateur-friendly, and easy to live with in an at-home setting.

When the seller (also his breeder and a veterinarian) volunteered specific examples, plus references, in response to Sue's questions, Sue asked for a video. She then shared it with her vet, trainer friends, and buddies. After gathering their (positive) input, she drove 8 hours to try the horse. What she found supported the seller's "sell."

She then arranged to haul the gelding off-site for a thorough prepurchase exam, so she could use the vet of her choice, see how well the horse hauled, and observe his temperament in a new setting. He passed all with flying colors. And Sue ended up with a horse that went on to earn an APHA World Championship and multiple Top 10 and Top 5 finishes in hunter events. That's a happy ending to Internet shopping…when it's done right.

DO

If you like what you hear about a specific horse, ask for a current video, then share it with your trainer or agent, your vet, horse friends—anyone who can offer an educated opinion.

■ **Call references.** Get numbers for the horse's veterinarian, farrier, and trainer (if applicable), and call every one of them. Ask about the horse's health/soundness history, the state of his feet, his level of training, attitude, and any vices. (What's that? The seller doesn't want to provide these numbers? Big RED FLAG! Move on to another prospect.)

■ **If everything still sounds good, ask for a video/DVD.** Then turn to Chapter 9: "Evaluating Sale Videos (DVDs)," page 69. If you like what you see, show it to your trainer or agent, your vet, your farrier, your knowledgeable friends—solicit as many opinions as you can find. (What's that? The seller doesn't have a video? Ask him or her to make one, offering to put down a deposit on it, if necessary. If he or she still won't make one, I'd be suspicious—they obviously aren't keen on selling the horse, or may be hiding something. If you're close enough to go see the horse without spending a lot of time and money, it may be worth a shot. Otherwise, I'd pass.)

■ **If the horse looks appealing...** Recruit your trainer or agent, and make an appointment to go see the horse. Then turn to Chapter 12 for help in evaluating him. If you like him, schedule a prepurchase exam (Chapter 14). If that works out, close the deal (Chapter 15). And enjoy!

Cyber-shopper savvy

$ **Set a budget and travel limit.** Before you start your search, nail down an exact budget and how far your time and budget will enable you to travel to see a potential buy. That way, you won't waste sellers' time by "tire-kicking" horses you can't afford, or can't go to see. Then take advantage of the sites that have advanced search engines (see "A Click Away," opposite page), which enable you to limit your search to a specific dollar amount, and to a specific state or distance from your zip code.

$ **Focus on keywords.** In the search engine, type in your target breed, gender, discipline, pedigree, and height. Some sites have their advanced search engines organized by such categories, so offer a list of pre-selected keywords you can choose from. (Some also offer color choices. But I'd highly recommend you look beyond color when shopping for the right horse!)

$ **Shop it.** Sure, you may not have the budget to travel from Seattle to Miami to look at a specific horse. But use the Web's wide reach to check pricing in different parts of the country for the type of horse you're targeting. Doing so will give you a feel for the market—and help you spot any too-good-to-be-true, or outrageously priced, horses.

$ **Work it.** When you find an interesting prospect, do a background check before you call the seller. If you're looking for a registered horse, verify that the horse *is* registered by using the association's online resource or by calling them. (For a list of breed and event associations, see page 25.) Also verify the current owner (which can alert you to any transfer issues), plus the horse's basic description (age, color, gender). You can also verify pedigree and performance claims.

$ **Be polite.** You can initially contact the seller via email. If the horse sounds good, make arrangements to contact the seller by phone, at a time convenient for him or her, so you can better size up the horse (and the seller). Be courteous and polite, but ask a lot of questions. Remember, the seller is sizing you up, too.

$ **Do as you say.** If you request a video or DVD be sent to you, and the seller asks you to return it, do it. (It's the people who don't return them that have forced some sellers to request deposits—of up to $50—before sending out a tape.) Fortunately, more and more sellers are taking advantage of online video services offered on horse-for-sale sites. While the quality may vary depending on your computer, expect such services to become much more available (and of increasing quality) to horse shoppers.

A Click Away

Here's a sampling of some current sites that can jump-start your horse search:

www.agdirect.com..........Large farm/ranch classified site with an all-breed, advanced search engine

www.barrelhorse.com ....Site for barrel racing classifieds and news

www.equine.com ....High-volume, all-breed site with advanced search engine

www.horsetrader.com ....Nationwide classifieds by the *California Horse Trader*

www.huntseathorses.com ....Site devoted to stock-breed hunt-seat horses

www.netequine.com ....Photo classifieds for all-breed horses/services

www.pleasurehorses.com..Dedicated to Western pleasure horses

www.qhd.com ....Quarter Horse directory with classifieds

If you're an inexperienced rider, avoid buying an inexperienced horse. You'll save both of you lots of frustration (and yourself potential injury).

CHAPTER 6

When Green Means No

Sure, you'll pay less up front for a young and/or inexperienced horse. But will you save in the long run?

6

> I'll keep this short and sweet. A green horse + a green rider = disaster. I've never seen a situation like that in which I've said, "Boy, I was wrong. That combination really worked."

"Sure he's green, but he was cheap."

"I hope your doctor's bills will be!"

It happens all the time: You start to feel pretty good about your riding and are thinking about buying a new horse. You may be graduating from lessons to a first horse, or buying a "step-up" horse on which to take your riding to another level. Either way, you make up your wish list and check around, quickly realizing that finding a sound, sane, seasoned, not-too-young and not-too-old horse in your price range is going to be a challenge. And, you begin to noodle with the idea of compromising, by buying one with a little less training. Or, perhaps, a lot less training.

I have one word for you: Whoa!

When you buy a new car, your wish list no doubt includes power steering, stereo, air conditioning, and perhaps a power seat. You don't shop for a stripped-down car then figure out how to add that stuff later, do you?

A green horse is the equivalent of that stripped-down car. Unless you're a master mechanic with the knowledge and resources to add the missing "options" easily and at a reasonable price, you'll be facing lots of frustration. And you may wreck the car.

> Unfortunately, many riders (especially inexperienced ones) resist asserting themselves, saying "I want my horse to like me." It's always good for a horse to like you. But it's critical that he respect you.

The frustration factor

I've seen so many people get frustrated because they bought a green horse—a horse that needed training and management that exceeded the rider's ability. Both parties lose.

Horses go through several stages when in training. They start out like a child just entering first grade at school. Most are open to learning what you'll be teaching, because it's new and different. Once you get past those initial lessons, though, a horse will have learned just enough to start trying to outthink you. He'll enter his "adolescence," figuring out that school can be hard and it's not always fun—just like most kids do.

At that point, you have to correct and reward him

Opposite Page: Young or inexperienced horses can be insecure—and reactive. Reactivity (such as a spook, like this one) can cause accidents, if you lack the experience or confidence to deal with it. *Above left:* You have to correct... *Above right:* ...and reward a green horse with the right balance in order to instill confidence and teach him how to behave, react, and respond, much as a parent does with a teenager. If you lack the feel to do this, you'll likely run into trouble.

with the right balance to maximize his ability and confidence and minimize disobedience, just like a parent will do raising a teenager that's testing his or her boundaries. With a horse, it takes lots of training, by showing him the right way to behave, react, and respond over and over and over until it becomes a habit. And that takes years of riding and exposure to different situations. I ride and haul young horses thousands of miles and spend years getting them broke. I know what it takes.

I've also worked with horses long enough to understand a critical aspect of horse behavior that many green riders don't: You can't get a horse to behave well by bribing him with treats or trying to be his best friend. As herd animals, they live by a pecking order—it's not a democracy. In other words, horses don't have equal relationships with other horses. In a herd of two, one will always be dominant, and the other submissive.

In your "herd of two" with any horse, you'll both be happier and safer if he acknowledges you as the boss hoss. (Think of it as a parent/child relationship. You can be buddies, but it's *you* who'll lay down and enforce the rules.) This is especially true with a green or young horse, whose lack of training can fuel insecurity. Insecurity can fuel reactivity. And reactivity can cause accidents. Unfortunately, many riders (especially inexperienced ones) resist asserting themselves, saying "I want my horse to like me." It's always good for a horse to like you. But it's critical that he respect you.

Ode to the older horse

Good, broke older horses are like handfuls of gold: They're a true treasure.

A good older horse is a treasure. He's got the experience and exposure to help you maximize your enjoyment. He can be not only a partner, but a mentor to you or your child, if you lack experience. And he'll be immediately ready to go do whatever it is you want to do.

So why do so many buyers bypass these treasures? I guess they worry the horse won't last, or will lose value too quickly. I disagree. If you choose carefully, and your prepurchase veterinarian tells you a seasoned horse will be serviceably sound for his intended job (see Chapter 14, page 125), why would you pass him up? Sure he might need some maintenance, but even young horses can need that. And they can break, too.

I have older horses in my barn that remain top performers. The youngest is 8 years old; the others are in the double digits, age-wise. Two are world champions and one has won a national honor roll title. These horses know their jobs, and are terrific schoolmasters for the amateurs who ride them. I treat each of them like a handful of gold: once you lose it, it's hard to find another one.

Are these horses still valuable? You bet. They'd be tough to replace. So do yourself a favor: Avoid bypassing such a treasure. And when you find one, treat him like the handful of gold that he is.

Green horse reality check

Here's what you need to know about the realities of working with green/young horses:

- **They require confident handling/riding.** If you allow horses to walk into your space, or worse, into you, you're not ready to work with a green horse. If you get butterflies in your belly even *thinking* about riding a young or inexperienced horse outside the safety of a round pen or arena, he's not for you.

- **They will misbehave.** Any green horse is going to test boundaries. This may be by intruding into your space on the ground, as mentioned above. Or it could be by resisting (or displaying exuberance) via a buck or other unexpected maneuver. If that kind of thing makes you nervous, green most definitely means no.

A young or green horse will misbehave and/or test boundaries. If that makes you nervous, opt for a broke one. You'll enjoy him more.

■ **They require time.** Most green horses need to be ridden five or six days a week in order to progress. If you're lucky, you can find one that can slip by with four. But for the average rider, getting on a green horse that hasn't been ridden for several days won't be much fun. And keep in mind that, unlike a pro, your time for horses can evaporate if family or work issues come up. Can you really commit to what a green horse needs?

■ **They require time, II.** Plan on at least two years of consistent training (see above) to get your horse broke. Even after that point, it takes time and consistency to maintain a successful partnership.

■ **They can require money.** Because many amateurs lack the time and/or facilities to ride and train a green horse, such horses often develop problems that require professional training to resolve. So the money you save buying a greenie can evaporate when you have to start paying training bills.

■ **They require experience.** Consistency is key. Every time a green horse is handled, he's being "trained." That means having the teenager next door work your horse isn't going to cut it, unless that teen is a confident, experienced rider.

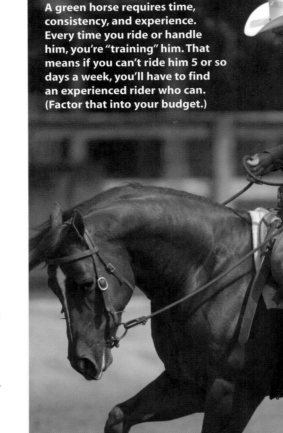

A green horse requires time, consistency, and experience. Every time you ride or handle him, you're "training" him. That means if you can't ride him 5 or so days a week, you'll have to find an experienced rider who can. (Factor that into your budget.)

■ **They require experience, II.** You have to know how to read a horse to work with a green one. For instance, do you have an innate feel for when to push a horse, and when to back off? Just like parenting, training requires intuition. Is the horse a smart, confident, quick learner who enjoys being challenged? Or a cautious type that thrives on routine? That's what amateurs pay trainers to know.

The last word

You may say, "We can't afford to buy a trained horse." To me, most people can't afford *not* to buy a trained one. How do you do it? Use these tips:

■ **Save longer:** Rather than compromising to get the wrong horse right now, hold off and save your money for a while longer, until you can afford a seasoned horse.

■ **Buy an older horse.** Don't shy away from older horses. A seasoned veteran with some mileage may require health maintenance, but if a prepurchase exam (see Chapter 14) determines that he's serviceably sound for your needs, he could be ideal. You can take an aged horse and improve him far more easily (and faster) than you can train a young or green one.

■ **Be realistic.** That yearling or 2-year-old may look appealing from a price standpoint, but don't forget to factor in a couple years' worth of feed, farrier, vet, and board bills, if applicable. Plus the likely training help you'll need. And the time.

Wouldn't you be better off counting up the money you'd spend on a young and/or green one, then using that money to invest in the *right* horse for your needs, even if you need to take out a loan? You'll get to begin enjoying the horse immediately, without spending time and money to try to "build" a horse that'll work out for you (or…not).

I'll say it again: For the average buyer, broke is better. You can instantly enjoy a seasoned horse, and improve him, if you want to, far more easily and faster than a young or green one. And that may make such a horse less expensive in the long run.

Your child's first horse or pony will set the tone for his or her future relationship (or lack of it) with equines. So be sure to shop smart so that first experience is a positive one.

CHAPTER 7

Shopping For
Your Kid's First Horse

Use these tips to choose a first horse for your child.

"This one's easy—buy your kid a quiet, experienced, older horse that has loads of good mileage. To buy a youngster a young horse would be like allowing your 5-year-old to be taught and supervised by another 5-year-old. No one's going to learn anything, and things could turn bad in a hurry.

Bob's Personal Experience

Your child has shown a genuine interest in horses and the responsibilities that go with them. Now she (or he) is asking for a horse of her own. You're worried you won't be able to find a horse you can trust with her—especially one you can afford. How do you *know* if a horse will be safe? And what will you have to pay for one that's kidproof?

Use these tips to find out.

1. Make sure your child is ready

Here's where a trainer/agent can really help. (To find one, see Chapter 3, page 19.) The assessment of a child's readiness should come from the trainer/agent and you, the parents, acting as a team.

While some kids start riding as early as 5 years of age (or earlier), some pros who work with kids encourage parents to begin with lessons when their child is about 8 or 9. Regardless of age, allowing the child to take lessons from a reputable trainer experienced with teaching children will allow you and the child to determine if her interest is real, or just a passing fancy. And it'll give the trainer an opportunity to evaluate the child's maturity, strength, and coordination.

Enrolling your child in a lesson program also gives her a chance to ride a variety of horses, which can teach her a great deal. And it gives you and your trainer a chance to observe her

A good lesson program is a fairly inexpensive way to enable your child to ride a lot of different horses, and allow his trainer to evaluate maturity, skills, and coordination. That way you'll know when the child is ready for a horse of his own.

readiness for a horse of her own. For instance, even at the age of 9 some kids aren't "big picture" ready when it comes to ownership. For example, will your child make sure her pony gets a thorough grooming before and after riding? Apply fly spray in the summer, and blankets in the winter? Keep her tack maintained without having to be constantly reminded? Pick up after herself at the barn?

Once a child has learned the basics, you can further test the waters with a lease or half-lease. That way, you can gauge your child's interest and commitment without making a big investment. If she remains committed, you can start shopping for a safe, experienced kid's horse.

2. What to look for in a "kidproof" first horse

For young children, a kind, quiet pony can make an ideal first horse. Size-wise, as his stature makes it easier for a kid to handle and groom him. It's also a shorter distance to the ground in the event of a fall.

When shopping, keep in mind these two words: Age and experience. An age between 15 and 20 is ideal, and a resume that reveals a solid history as a kid's pony is mandatory. That way, you know the pony should be past any youthful exuberance, and has the mileage to make him a mentor and teacher. A pony that's arthritic is okay, too—slow movement is ideal for a child just learning to ride.

Some people hate ponies. Yes, they can be naughty, and you may have to look at a lot of them to find the right one. But a decent pony or small horse can be less intimidating to a child than a larger horse. And if a pony happens to kick, he's not packing 1,200 pounds of horsepower behind him. A small child may be able to saddle and bridle a pony by herself, too.

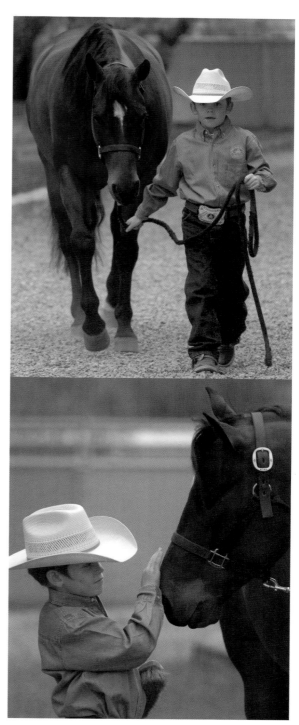

Top: An older (aged 15 to 20) small horse or pony with lots of kid mileage can make an ideal first horse. *Above:* When shopping, look for a horse that has kids hanging all over him, indicating a high tolerance for children.

For an older child, a horse that fits the
same age/experience criteria would work
well. Choose one that's suitable, size-wise,
to your child. Look, too, for horses that
may have been retired from the show ring.
Such horses will be broke and have a lot of
good mileage. You want your child to learn
from the horse—not the other way around.

3. Where to find good kids' horses

Your child's trainer can help you. A barn
that caters to kids can be a great source for
horses that are outgrown physically or
because their kid is ready for the next level
of horse. Such horses often get passed from
child to child via word of mouth, so let
others at the barn know you're looking.

Kid-oriented shows
and barns are a great
place to find kid-
proof horses, which
are often passed from
child to child via word
of mouth.

Another good place to find kids' horses
and ponies is at small, local, kid-oriented horse shows, such as those put on by 4-H clubs or Pony
Clubs. Even if you never plan for your kid to show, the equines you find at such events are usually
ridden by dedicated kids who pile the miles on them.

The fact that a horse is at the show means he likely hauls, ties, can be clipped, etc. Look for the
horse or pony that has kids hanging all over him, indicating a high level of tolerance for children.
Also look for one whose owner has obviously outgrown him, as indicated by the kid's legs hanging
below the pony's belly.

Smart buyer tip:

When you go to try a child's horse, leave your child at home, to keep him or her from
getting too attached to a horse that could turn out to be inappropriate.

And, take along an older, experienced kid to test out the horse. Some horses will
behave perfectly for an adult rider, but get bratty when they sense a child on board.

Avoid being influenced by color, breed, or gender when shopping for your kid's first horse. You want to buy a wise, quiet mentor—not Trigger!

4. How much can you expect to pay?

If you can lease a first horse, you can often do so for the cost of monthly board, plus lessons. Some owners will even pay vet and farrier bills, though others will ask you to do so. And some leases do charge a "for profit" fee on top of expenses. Others may require a one-year lease, not including lessons. Annual fees can range from $3,500 and up.

To buy a children's horse, expect to pay from around $2,000 to about $12,000 (or more). The low end generally covers a horse that'll be used purely for recreation. The upper range is for one that will some day be shown, so requires show experience with kids. You may also luck out and find a seasoned show horse whose owners are looking to place him in a good home. In that case, you may pay less, or even nothing. Expect the owners to check out you and your facilities thoroughly, though, before giving you the horse.

Some parents take a proactive approach, by placing ads specifying exactly what they want in a kid's horse, then plastering the ads locally, in barns and feed/tack stores.

5. Test the horse's or pony's kid-proofness

First, see the "Smart Buyer Tip," page 56, about leaving your little horseperson behind when you go to see a horse. Then, before you go see the horse, call the owner and ask for several previous owners, then call them and run through the "Smart Buyer Questionnaire," page 91. When you do

Common parental mistakes

- **Knowing little or nothing about horses,** and shopping for a horse without experienced help. (A potential disaster for your child.)

- **Emphasizing color over suitability for your child.** You'd be amazed at how many parents want to buy their kid Trigger.

- **Emphasizing breed over suitability.** Breed bias commonly makes parents pass over ideal horses and ponies.

- **Emphasizing gender over suitability.** Each horse should be judged as an individual.

go see him, watch how the horse behaves around his current kid when being handled, groomed, tied, etc. (For a thorough look at how to evaluate a horse in person, see Chapter 12: "Smart Buyer Test-Ride Guide," page 95.)

And watch the kid. Does he act afraid of the horse or pony? Is the horse aggressive, pinning his ears or swishing his tail?

The bottom line: Your child's first horse or pony will set the tone for her relationship with any future equines. Shop smart so you make it a safe and positive experience for her. You'll all benefit.

Take an experienced child with you to test ride the horse; many horses will behave well for adults, but not tolerate children. Then take the horse away from his familiar area and watch his reactions. Is he mellow, or tense? And ask yourself this: Would you trust him with your own flesh-and-blood on board?

The bottom line: Your child's first horse or pony will set the tone for her relationship with any future equines. Shop smart so you make it a safe and positive experience for her. You'll all benefit.

A cribber like this one is hard for you to watch and listen to, but the habit doesn't really affect his wellbeing. However, it could affect your ability to resell him.

CHAPTER 8

Vice Squad

Here are 28 common vices or habits you may—or may not—consider living with in a new horse.

"If you haven't spent a living shopping for horses like I have, it can be easy to over-look a problem. (That's why I suggest you spend a little bit of extra money and hire an expert to help you shop; see Chapter 3.)

I've seen so many "experienced" amateur horse people end up with a horse that has a habit or vice the buyer didn't discover until he or she got the horse home. Why? If you're not familiar with what to look for (or how a seller can camouflage a problem), you may miss it.

For instance, I know one 20-something gal who's a terrific rider on a national level. She doesn't have a regular trainer, preferring to haul to pros when she needs help. She and her mother spent months shopping for just the right horse to take the girl to the next level—without professional help.

And they found what seemed to be the perfect gelding. He was living outside in a big paddock because the barn was "full." The girl and her mother never thought to observe the horse in a stall; even though he was to be a show horse, and would be stalled at home and at shows.

Imagine their surprise when they discovered…after they'd bought him and brought him home…that he's a wicked-bad stall (and trailer) kicker. It makes boarding and showing him (not to mention hauling him) a major challenge.

I could list many more similar examples, but you get the picture. Shopping for horses is truly a buyer-beware experience! If the good way outweighs the bad, you might buy a horse with a fairly benign habit or vice. But I recommend that you ask yourself this question: Would you set out to buy a car with a problem? I don't think so."

Just like people, horses can develop bad habits. Some may be harmful to their wellbeing; some may be relatively harmless, but can cause management headaches for you.

How do you uncover a problem in a horse you're looking at? Use these tips:

■ **Ask the seller to tell you** *everything* **he or she knows about the horse, good and bad.** Tell him or her not to be shy about "the bad," since you'd like to make an informed decision. (See "Smart Buyer Questionnaire," page 91.) Listen to what he or she says, then conduct your own checks (keep reading!).

■ **Ask to see the horse in a variety of circumstances,** particularly the way you'll house him if you were to buy him. For instance, if the horse will be stalled, ask to observe his behavior in a stall. Does he crib? Kick the walls? Weave? (For info on these problems, see the chart on page 64.)

Then enter the stall. Does the horse turn to greet you with his ears up and eyes soft? Or does he pin his ears and/or turn tail? If you'll house him in a pen or pasture, can he be easily caught out in the open?

■ **Ask to see him load in a trailer.** (After all, if he doesn't load, how the heck will you get him home?) Then ask the seller to haul him around the block. Does the horse kick the trailer walls? Scramble around corners?

■ **Ask to see the horse tied and cross-tied.** Does he stand quietly while tied, patiently awaiting your next move? Or does he paw, squirm, or try to set back and break the restraint?

■ **Ask to observe him being saddled and bridled.** Does he stand quietly? Or does he resist the process, pinning his ears and turning around to bite at his handler at every opportunity?

If you'll be riding the horse, ride him in a variety of areas to test his temperament. (For more information, see Chapter 12, page 95.) If you ever feel fearful, watch out. If a horse scares you in his home environment, he may terrify you in a new environment (yours).

Don't be shy: For several common (and fixable) problems, such as trailer-loading issues or a

"How is he in a stall? Why, he's perfect!"

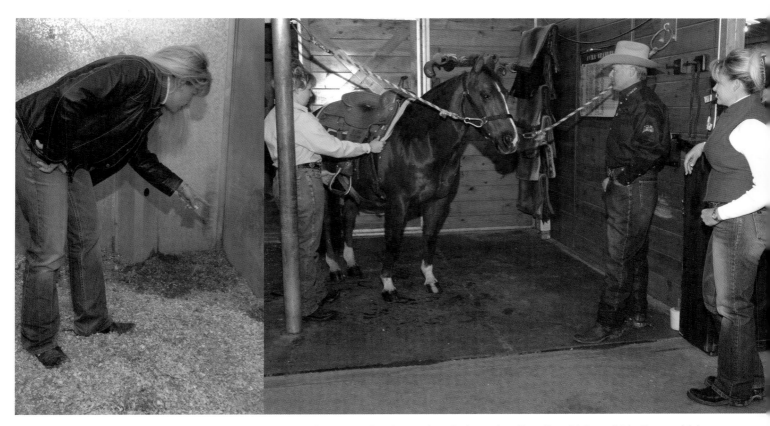

Above left: Look around the horse's stall for signs of a vice, such as indented stall walls, which could indicate a kicker. **Above right:** How a horse stands (or doesn't!) while tied or in cross-ties, and as he's being saddled, can tell you a lot about his personality.

Cribbing is when a horse grabs a solid object and sucks in air. It's habit-forming for horses because it causes an endorphin release.

horse that's hard to catch, if you like the horse a lot, ask the seller to work on the problem. If he or she is motivated to sell, he'll/she'll realize it's worth the time to fix it. You can then make a return visit and finalize your decision to buy, or not to buy.

Following is a list of 28 common vices/habits you may come across while shopping. For each, I've included what it is, why it can occur, whether it can be fixed, and whether I'd take the risk on a horse. As you'll see, in some cases I will take the risk, for many I'd suggest such a horse only for experienced hands, and some I wouldn't take a risk on at all.

In the stall

Vice/Habit	What you see	Why it occurs	Fixable?	Worth the risk?
Turns tail	Greets you with his kicking gear when you approach.	Can be territoriality, dominance, or fear-related.	Maybe.	Probably not; for experienced handlers only.
Attacks stall bars	Rushes with teeth bared as you approach stall.	Can be territoriality- or dominance-related.	Maybe.	I'd pass; that's an attitude (and problem) I don't want in my barn.
Pins ears	Flattens ears when you approach/handle.	Can be a sign of a cranky attitude indicating dislike of people or job.	Maybe.	Slight pinning of ears is probably okay; if horse pins ears when you halter him, I'd probably pass—he's not going to be fun to work with.
Kicks wall	Lets one or both hind legs fly at feeding or other times.	Can be due to territoriality and/or confinement issues.	Can be tough to cure, and can damage horse's legs (and stall).	Probably not.
Chews wood	You see signs the horse gnaws wood surfaces.	Boredom; lack of "chew time" (hay/grass); in young horses, teething.	Can be, with increased exercise/roughage, and making wood surfaces less palatable, or covering with metal; youngster likely will outgrow.	Probably.
Cribs	Grabs solid surface with teeth and sucks in air.	Can be due to confinement and/or isolation issues.	Not really; can be managed with a cribbing collar.	If buying for resale, no; if buying to keep for yourself, and all else is good, yes (cribbing is worse to watch and listen to than it is on the horse's wellbeing).
Weaves	Rhythmically sways back and forth with front legs.	Can be due to confinement/isolation.	Can possibly be managed with a horse-safe stall mirror, and/or switch to pasture living.	Probably not, especially if he'll live in a stall; weaving is hard on the legs and can cause weight loss.

When tied/cross-tied

Vice/Habit	What you see	Why it occurs	Fixable?	Worth the risk?
Sets back	Fights against restraint in an effort to get free when tied.	Poor training or a bad experience, resulting in panic when restrained.	It can be; it can also be unsafe for you and the horse.	If you're a pro and all else is good, maybe; if you're not a pro, why go there?
Kicks	When you approach, lifts a hind leg in your general direction, or actually lashes out with it.	Can be territoriality- or dominance-related.	Doesn't matter: the answer is…	…NO!
Bites	Tries to grab a piece of you with his teeth whenever you're near his head.	Can be territoriality- or dominance-related.	As with kicking, it doesn't matter to me, the answer is…	…NO!
Paws	Slaps or digs at the ground with one front foot.	Bored and/or impatient.	Maybe.	Not desirable, but not a deal breaker in my book.

When caught/led

Vice/Habit	What you see	Why it occurs	Fixable?	Worth the risk?
Hard to catch	Horse won't allow you to walk up to him in pasture/paddock.	Can be resistance due to anticipation of work.	Probably.	Not a deal breaker, if all else is good, but it is undesirable; ask sellers to work on before you buy horse.
Head shy	Raises head/pulls away when you try to halter (or bridle).	Fear, improper training, and/or bad experience; it's a man-made problem.	Yes.	Yes, if the problem isn't to the point it puts you or the horse in danger.
Drags behind	When led, makes you pull him along, rather than willingly walking beside you.	Lack of training.	Yes.	If all else is good, probably.
Pulls ahead	Drags *you* along when you try to lead.	Lack of training.	Yes.	If all else is good, probably.

When caught/led (continued)

Vice/Habit	What you see	Why it occurs	Fixable?	Worth the risk?
Herd bound	Resists being led away from barn/buddies.	Insecurity—fears leaving "herd."	Can be, but is a sign of an insecure horse.	Unless you're a pro or highly experienced hand, I'd pass.
Spooky	Horse spooks when led past a "scary" object, or hears a sudden noise.	Can be age-related; fairly typical for young (3 years and below), inexperienced horses; in older horse can be due to heightened "flight" response.	Depends on age/temperament.	If it's a mature horse and you want one you can relax with at home, shows, or on the trail, no; if it's a young-ster, and you lack experi-ence, well that's a no, too.

When saddled/ridden

Vice/Habit	What you see	Why it occurs	Fixable?	Worth the risk?
Cinchy	When cinch/girth is tightened, horse snakes head around and threatens to bite, and/or humps back and kicks out/bucks.	Can be a pain response (conditioned from a current or past injury), or resistance/improper training.	Maybe.	If the horse just acts slightly irritated (briefly pins ears/raises head), he's prob-ably okay; if he humps back or bucks/kicks out, a defi-nite no—such behaviors can lead to bucking or rearing under saddle.
Rearing	Horse resists forward movement, bouncing front legs off ground, and/or actually rears, standing on hind legs.	Can be fear-, resistance-, evasion- and/or poor-training related.	Maybe not.	NO! I wouldn't buy a horse that's reared for any reason (and I always ask a seller if the horse has)—he can flip over and kill you; to me, once they've reared, there's always a risk they'll do it again.
Bucking	Horse humps back and kicks out with hind legs under saddle.	Can be due to freshness, fear (often following a spook), or resistance.	Depends on the cause.	For a kid's, novice, or family horse, no; if it's a 2-year-old with 30 days under saddle, and you're a pro, maybe; if the horse is billed as "broke," there's no excuse.

Vice/Habit	What you see	Why it occurs	Fixable?	Worth the risk?
Pushy	Horse steps into you/your space as you saddle him.	Lack of respect due to bad attitude or poor training.	Maybe.	If horse shows other signs of disrespect (pinned ears; turned tail/threats to kick), NO; if horse is young/green but otherwise agreeable, maybe (but this is one of my pet peeves—I don't like pushy horses…they can be dangerous).
Herd bound/ barn sour	Resists being ridden away from barn/buddies.	Fears leaving "herd."	Maybe, but such a horse can be dangerous if you lack experience.	Unless you're a seasoned pro or highly experienced hand, I'd pass.
Tail wringing	Horse wrings/swishes tail (and probably pins ears) when you apply an aid/cue.	Pain, irritation, poor training, rider error.	Maybe not, once engrained.	Tail wringing is a sign of an unhappy horse, and is unattractive, to boot; I'd probably pass.
Kicks/bites when passing	Lashes out at other horses when passing.	Territoriality/dominance issues, and/or an attitude problem.	May not be.	I'd pass: such a horse is a liability; he could seriously injure another horse—or rider.

In a trailer

Vice/Habit	What you see	Why it occurs	Fixable?	Worth the risk?
Loading problems	Either resists or refuses being loaded.	May have been frightened or improperly trained.	Yes.	If you *really* like the horse, tell seller you'll come back when the horse has learned how to load properly—but not before.
Kicks trailer	Once loaded and while hauling, kicks trailer wall.	Can be territoriality- or confinement-related.	Some cases can be managed with hobbles; hard to fix (and hard on horse/trailer!).	Not unless you're a pro and have the experience (and equipment) to deal with the problem.
Paws trailer	Paws with front foot, especially when trailer is stopped.	Can be confinement-related, or sign of impatience.	Hard to fix.	Probably, if all else is good; more of an annoyance, especially if horse only paws when trailer has stopped.
Scrambles	Horse flails around when you take a corner.	Can be panic due to confinement and/or perceived loss of balance.	Some horses respond to a change in trailer configuration (such as from straight- to slant-load); otherwise, tough to fix.	If all else is good and the horse rides well in *your* trailer type, probably; if not, I'd pass.

A good video can make a mediocre horse look good, and a bad video can make a great horse look mediocre. Use videos as a shopping tool, but they're no substitute for a hands-on look.

CHAPTER 9

Evaluating Sales Videos (DVDs)

Here's what a horse-for-sale video can (and can't) tell you.

"I've seen thousands of sale videos. Personally, I find them helpful to a certain point, but they don't take the place of seeing a horse in the flesh. That's because a good video can make a mediocre horse look great, and a bad video (and there are lots of them) can make a great horse look mediocre.

For instance, I recently watched a painfully bad video of a young gray Quarter Horse stallion. Not flattering at all. But I liked the horse's looks, breeding, and color enough to go see him in person. He was a way better horse than the video revealed, and I bought him.

Conversely, I've seen horses that look world-class on tape, and not nearly so impressive in person. My advice? Keep an open mind…but don't be fooled. Nothing in horse buying is as valuable as going to see, touch, and ride the horse yourself."

Bob's Personal Experience

9

Many sellers have realized the value of having a video available when selling a horse. Videos ratchet up responses to an ad (either print or Internet) by giving prospective buyers a chance to view the horse in action without having to drive or fly.

That's why more and more ads (and even word-of-mouth sellers) have the tagline "video available." You may have to pay a deposit to some sellers, which can range from about $10 to $50, to have a video sent. To me, if you're truly interested in a horse, it's worth it. (And if you return the video, you may get your deposit back.) Most sellers do this to weed out the "tire kickers" who love to look but never buy.

A good sales video will contain the following:

■ **Conformation views.** Profile shots from both sides, as well as the front and back, plus a close-up of the horse's head, feet, and legs.

■ **Movement from the front/back.** The horse being led or ridden at the walk and jog directly away from and back toward the camera, so you can evaluate correctness of movement from the front and back.

■ **Movement from the side.** The horse being ridden (if he's broke) or longed in both directions at the walk, jog, and lope.

Above left: A good video will have a profile shot so you can evaluate the horse's conformation and balance from the side.
Above right: It'll also contain shots of the horse's front and back legs, and have him move to and from the camera so you can see if he tracks straight.

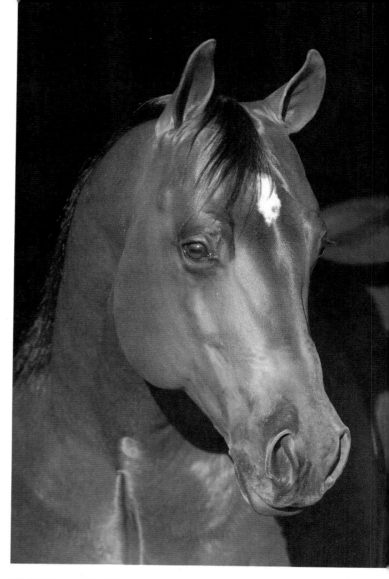

- **Specialized maneuvers.** If the horse is a hunter or jumper, the tape should (hopefully) include him being jumped around a course, or at least over several fences. (If he's not yet broke to ride, he may be free jumped.) If he's a reiner or pattern horse, he'll be shown performing specific maneuvers, such as stops, turnarounds, and lead changes. A cow horse will be shown working cattle; a trail horse may be shown negotiating water or logs.

- **Show footage.** Video of the horse in the show ring, if he's a show horse.

Some motivated sellers will shoot a video to your specifications if theirs doesn't include something you'd like to see, especially if they determine you're serious about a horse. If that's the case, consider asking to see the following, in addition to any specific maneuvers or performance footage: the horse being loaded and unloaded, tied, clipped, tacked up, or any other task that reveals manners and attitude.

When you look at a sales video, use these tips to glean the most from it:

1. Looks. Do you like your first impression of the horse?

Watch for:

An overall attractive, appealing horse. This is especially critical if you'll be selling him yourself at some point—pretty sells. Also look for a big, soft eye and kind

Top: A gorgeous head and kind, soft eye will not only make the horse attractive to you, but will make him easy to market if you sell him yourself at some point. ***Above:*** The video should show footage of the horse being ridden or longed so you can evaluate his movement.

expression, which can be indicators of a willing attitude. (Small, hard, pinched eyes are something I run from. In my experience, horses that have them can be tough to work with.)

Proper condition. Is he too thin, which could indicate a lack of proper care (and future health issues), or a horse that's high-strung and hard to keep weight on? Too fat, which could indicate a lack of work (not good if you want a riding horse…why isn't he working)? Or just right (not too thin, not too fat)?

> If you like what you see on the tape (or are unsure), show it to a reputable trainer or agent, your veterinarian, farrier, and knowledgeable friends. The more opinions you get at this point, the better.

Conformation. Does he look balanced? By that, I mean do his neck, back, and hip lengths compliment each other, as well as the length and angle of his shoulder and hip? Or does he look like two different horses glued together in the middle? Are his legs straight and correct? His hooves healthy and balanced, without any corrective-type shoeing (such as a wedge or bar shoe, which could indicate a problem)?

2. Movement. Do you like the way the horse moves? From the front and back views, does the horse track perfectly straight with his front and hind legs, or do they swing in or out?

Corrective shoes such as those shown here could indicate a foot problem.

From the side, do his feet and legs appear to sweep forward, rhythmically and softly touching the ground, indicating good, correct movement (and the potential for a comfortable ride)? Or do they go up and down like pistons, slapping the ground in short, jarring, uneven strides? If it's the latter, I'd pass. How fun could that be to ride? (And how athletic could such a horse be?)

If the video doesn't include specialized maneuvers (such as this turnaround for a reiner), ask the seller to shoot some footage and send it to you. If he's motivated, he'll do that, plus any additional footage you'd like to see.

Pinned ears and a sour expression, such as that shown here, could indicate an attitude problem.

3. Suitability. Does the horse appear suitable for your chosen event? For instance, if you're looking for a pleasure horse, does he have a flat topline and tailset, or does his head stick up in the air, and his tail naturally flag out behind? If you're looking for a cow horse, does he look compact and athletic, versus tall and gangly? For a hunter, is he tall and elegant, versus short and bulky?

4. Attitude. This is one of the most important things you may be able to learn from a video. Study it: Does the horse look kind, relaxed, and respectful toward his handlers at all times? Does he lead

Before: "He sure looks good on the tape, Earl—let's buy him!"

After: "This can't be the horse on the tape!"

willingly, stand quietly to be saddled up and mounted, and go around with his ears up, his tail quiet, and a pleasant expression on his face? Or, is he cranky, resistant, and/or pushy, pinning his ears, dragging behind or charging ahead when led, refusing to stand still, pushing into his handler's space, tossing his head, wringing his tail, grinding his teeth, or showing any other sign of irritation and/or disrespect? If you see any, say no thanks!

5. Lameness. Do you see any signs of a head-bob when the horse moves, indicating lameness in a limb? Or does he appear to take a short-strided step with a leg or legs? If so, send the tape back and keep shopping.

The more eyes, the better

If you like what you see on the tape (or are unsure), show it to a reputable trainer or agent, your veterinarian, farrier, and knowledgeable friends. The more opinions you get at this point, the better. If you determine the horse is worth a test ride, schedule one, then turn to Chapter 12 on page 95.

If you don't, return the tape and move on. And be thankful it saved you the time and/or expense of having to go see the horse in person!

How a horse handles the crowds, noise, and excitement while being led to the sale ring and handled in it will provide valuable insights into his temperament.

Getting **professional** help

As you can see in this chapter, it takes work to make a good buy at auction. While my 7-Step strategy can help you make the process satisfactory, you may lack the experience or desire to tackle a sale on your own. Hiring a reputable trainer or agent, one with experience buying at sales, can help.

To find one, see Chapter 3: "How (And Why) To Get Help From A Pro." What you'll pay can vary. I charge around $500 to scout, research, and buy horses for clients. I know exactly where to look, who to talk to, and the right questions to ask.

The agent you choose can provide the same service for you. He or she may charge a flat fee, or a percentage (no more than 5 percent of the purchase price at a sale is fairly standard), plus expenses. Like a prepurchase exam, that's money well spent, since it can save you money—and heartache—in the long run.

—*Doug Carpenter*

companies, these sales showcase top breeders, owners, trainers, and competitors. You can bet sellers bring good stock to them.

However, there are good sales that aren't associated with major events, such as those that specialize in selling ranch or riding horses. (One such sale is put on by Horsebreakers Unlimited, which sells a variety of riding horses; www.horsebreakers.com. There are other, similar companies that hold sales.) Use the steps below to help find one, and to be a smart horse buyer when you go to a sale.

Step 1: Have a specific type of horse in mind

The best way to avoid getting caught up in the excitement of a sale—and buying a horse you don't need, or one that isn't suitable—is to go with a specific purpose. List exactly what type of horse you want (see Chapter 2: "Meet Your Match," for how to narrow down your specific needs), by writing your future horse's job description, and what it'll take to fill it.

List the features that are key to you, such as a certain size, age, temperament, level of training, show experience, and the like. Also list what you *don't* want, such as a cribber.

Get to the sale early so you can observe the horses being unloaded in a new setting, and handled. You'll be able to see which horses handle it well (a big thumbs up), and which ones don't (a big thumbs down).

Then write down in bold print exactly what your budget is, that is, the top dollar you can spend for this horse. Look at the sale as a way to fill this specific "order" for yourself.

Step 2: Find a good sale

No two horses are alike. And no two sales are, either. Some have good management and reputations; others don't.

■ **Select a sale that features the type of horse you want.** If you're looking for a specific breed, find a sale that's held in association with a major breed event, such as a world show. If you're looking for a specific event horse, such as a reiner, opt for a sale held in conjunction with a major reining event, such as the National Reining Horse Association's Breeders Showcase Sale. If you want a ranch horse, look for ranch horse sales.

■ **Choose a catalogued sale.** Such sales provide a catalog listing each sale horse's information, which allows you to do your research when you're still at home. (More on this in a minute.) These sales tend to advertise more extensively than a local auction, so will attract more high-quality horses to choose from. They also almost always have a veterinarian on hand to provide prepurchase exams.

■ **Ask around.** To locate a good sale, ask reputable friends, trainers, breeders, farriers, and veterinarians to recommend one for the type of horse you're looking for. In particular, ask each person if he or she has bought a horse from a specific sale, and whether it was a good experience.

Step 3: Order the sale catalog

Once you've selected a sale, call and request a catalog as far in advance as possible. Go through the catalog and put a check by any horses that meet your Step 1 criteria. Call the appropriate breed association, or go on-line for complete pedigree and performance records on the horses you choose, if applicable. (For a list of breed associations and their contact information, see Chapter 3: "How (And Why) To Get Help From A Pro.")

Many sales firms will provide you with a consigner's phone number, so you can call to get more info on a horse that interests you. If the consigner is local, ask to make an appointment to see his or her consignments before the sale. That way you can not only evaluate a horse, but also the environment and people that produced him. The more information you gather, the less likely you are to make a buying mistake.

Step 4: Get to the sale early

The early bird learns the most. Here's what you'll get:

- **A first look.** By arriving as soon as the grounds open for sale horses, you can get a behind-the-scenes look at the horses' demeanor as they're unloaded and handled in a new environment. You don't want anything that's bad-minded, hard to handle, or unsound. You'd be surprised what this first look can reveal. You'll also get to see the horses in their "natural state"—before they're slicked and shined for a trip to the sales ring, and how they tolerate such tasks as getting bathed and clipped.

Left: You'll find your terms-of-sale agreement at the sales office. Read it carefully before signing.
Right: Ask, too, for a stall chart, so you can find (and observe) the prospects you've picked.

■ **A "terms of sale" agreement.** Head to the sales office and get a copy. Read it fully before signing and getting your bidder's number. (It's your responsibility to know the rules and terms, and accept them, before you ever bid.)

Ask, too, if there are any supplements or substitutions, which are horses that entered the sale too late to be catalogued. (*Tip:* These horses will most likely be placed at the end of the sale, so could be some of the better buys.)

■ **A stall chart.** Ask for one at the sales office. Use it to find which consignments are in what stalls. That way you can save time in locating the horses you want to inspect closely. You'll also avoid getting distracted by those that don't fit your criteria.

Step 5: Inspect, inspect, inspect

Now go scope out your horses of interest. Don't be shy or reserved—this is an interactive process. You'll want to handle your prospects, and get as much info from the sellers as possible. Here's what to do:

■ **Watch, look, and listen.** Start out by standing back and observing the horse in his stall. Is he relaxed and quiet? Eating and drinking? Is his bedding relatively undisturbed? Those are all good signs that he's handling the new environment well.

Or, is he refusing to eat and drink? Pacing, whinnying, or stressed? If his bedding is trampled, that's evidence of nervous movement. (*Tip:* In my experience, a horse that's nervous in his stall is going to have a tendency to be nervous everywhere.)

Does he chew, crib, kick, weave, or squeal at nearby horses? Does he charge or pin his ears at humans or horses walking by the stall? Are his eyes bright and healthy? That's good. If they're dull and glassy, with a sunken look, accompanied by a head-down demeanor, it could indicate that he's been drugged or is ill.

Does he have any obvious blemishes, swellings, or injuries? If so, make note of them.

■ **Ask questions.** Pull out your "Smart Buyer Questionnaire" (see page 91). Let "any" be your operative word when asking

Left: Learn by watching: Observing a horse in his stall can tell you a lot. For instance, is he relaxed and quiet, as this horse is, or pacing and restless (a negative)? *Right:* You can also uncover some unpleasant habits by taking the time to watch. For instance, this horse may be a cribber.

Find the owner and ask a lot of questions. Don't be shy—now's your chance, before you bid. Here, Doug (middle) and Bob (right) ask the owner/consigner about this horse.

In my experience, a horse that's nervous in his stall is going to have a tendency to be nervous everywhere.

about such issues as soundness and behavior. In other words, "Has he had *any* lameness issues? Any health problems? Any bad habits?"

Here are other sample questions that can provide insights:

"How long have you owned the horse?" A short ownership period could indicate the seller bought the horse for re-sale—or had a problem with him.

"How's the horse been here?" If the seller tells you the horse is quiet at home, but has been a bit nervous at the sale, that makes sense. But if he tells you the horse is quiet here and nervous at home, that's a red flag that something's not right—you're not getting the straight story.

"Tell me everything that's good about this horse." Check the answers against your "want" list. If they match up, great. If not, move on to your next prospect.

"Tell me everything that's bad." If the seller says, "There's nothing bad," that's a red flag. Every horse has some kind of issue. What I want to hear is something that makes sense, such as, "If you don't ride him for a couple of days, you may want to longe him before you get on." That's reasonable—and realistic.

"What's he like to bridle and saddle?"

"Do you need to longe him every time you ride, or can you just get on and go?"

"What are his stall habits?"

"Can you turn him out with other horses?"

"Is he easy to catch?"

■ **Use the "Columbo approach."** Don't just ask these questions once on the horses you're looking at. Go back a couple of hours later and watch the horse some more, asking the same questions. I call it the "Columbo approach." You can say, "Forgive me if I've already asked…." The responses you'll get say a lot. If the seller's story changes, that's a red flag. For instance, if at first he or she says the horse stands perfectly for the farrier, but later the seller says, "Well, he can be tough to shoe behind," that's a clue that you're not getting the whole story. The horse may have other holes the seller is hiding.

Note any changes in the horse on your second visit. Did he go from dull to hyper alert? That may indicate he's emerging from a drug-induced calm. Is he the same? That's a good sign. Do you like him even better upon viewing him a second time? That's another good sign. If you like him less, note it. Stop by again, and if he's getting farther and farther from your short list, scratch him off.

■ **Get hands-on.** If you like what you see and hear, ask the owner if you can go in the stall. Then observe how the horse behaves with these in-stall tests:

Your approach: Does he greet you with

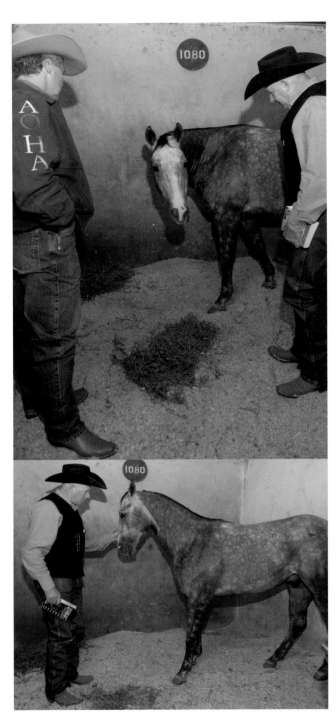

Top: A horse that greets you in the stall with polite, respectful interest, like this horse is, gets a thumbs-up. ***Above:*** When you apply pressure to a horse's nose, does he bend at the poll and step back? If so, that's good. If he braces and balks, he'll probably do the same when you apply cues when you ride him.

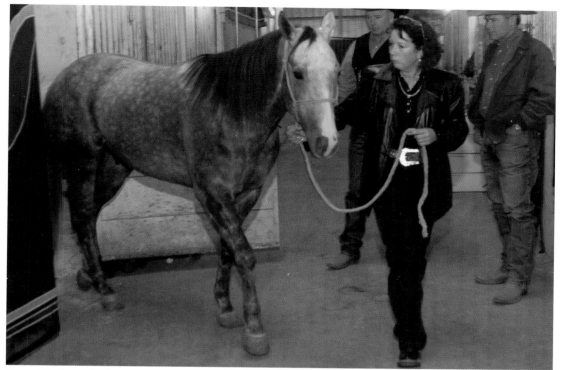

If you like how the horse acts in the stall, ask the seller to take him out so you can get a better look.

polite, ears-up interest, respectfully staying out of your space? If so, he gets a thumbs up. However, if he pins his ears, swishes his tail, pushes into you, or turns tail, that's a no-deal thumbs down. Move on.

Acceptance of pressure. Assuming he passes the approach test, run your hands over him to check his reaction. Does he calmly accept your touch? Or does he pin his ears and swish his tail (thumbs down!).

Then place a hand on his face, about where a noseband or bosal would go, and push against him (as shown in the photo at left). Does he yield at the poll? If so, that's a good indication of an accepting disposition—and a thumbs up. However, if he braces against your hand and/or tosses his head to resist the pressure, that's a major thumbs down. Chances are you'll get the same response when you ask him to yield to pressure under saddle.

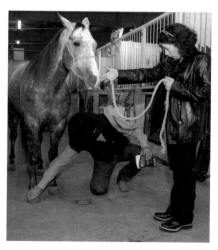

Having the horse stand on a firm, flat surface will enable you to carefully evaluate his conformation, and check his feet and legs.

■ **Observe him outside of the stall.** If you really like what you see so far, ask the seller to take him out of the stall and stand him on a hard, level surface so you can clearly evaluate

When you're ready to buy, don't be afraid to bid early on a horse you've researched and like. This makes your interest clear to the auctioneer.

his conformation, including feet and legs. Watch, too, how the horse behaves as he's being haltered and handled.

Run your hands over his legs to check for heat, swelling, or other problems. If you still like what you see, ask the seller to take the horse to an area where he can be worked, so you can further assess his attitude, plus his movement and ability.

If he's had training under saddle, ask for a demonstration. Refer to the previous chapters in this book for what to look for, including attitude as he's being saddled and bridled. See especially Chapter 12, page 95, for how to evaluate a horse on the ground and under saddle. If you'll be riding the horse, ask to ride him. If the owner refuses, be wary.

Step 6: Schedule a prepurchase exam

Assuming you like everything you've seen so far, order a prepurchase exam (PPE) for your top pick or picks, including x-rays, from the sale's attending veterinarian. Expect to pay between $500 and $800 for such an exam at a sale. But that's money well spent. In the long run, I've saved way more on PPE's by avoiding horses with problems, than I've spent on them. For more information, see Chapter 14: "The Prepurchase Exam," page 125.

If the horse is broke, ask to see him worked as part of your research. If he's a youngster, ask to see him longed, if he knows how, so you can evaluate movement (and further observe temperament). If not, have the seller move him at the walk and trot on the lead, as this one is doing.

Step 7: Bid...and buy (but stay cool)

If your picks pass the vet, prioritize your choices, listing them in order of preference and noting where they appear in the sale lineup. Decide what to do if your second-choice horse comes in before your first-choice horse. If you'll bid, note what you'd be willing to pay for that horse, versus your top choice.

Here are some other tips for successful bidding...and buying:

■ **Don't stop observing.** Go back to the stalls before your short-listed horses are due in the sale ring, then watch how each horse behaves when he's led to the ring. How he handles the crowds, noise, and excitement will provide valuable insights into his brain.

Do NOT let your friends or family talk you into overspending on a horse.

Don't be afraid to bid early. This makes your interest clear to the auctioneer and his bid spotters, or ringmen, whose job is to recognize bids and confirm them to the auctioneer. Things can move fast; if you wait too late to bid, you could miss out on a horse.

If you miss on a particular horse, worry not. There will always be another horse, and another sale. Trust me.

■ **Keep track of the bids.** At the sales I attend, an electronic tote board behind the auctioneer's stand lists bid increments as they occur. (This board also has a light-up feature to indicate whether a bred mare is actually in foal, and whether a horse is a cribber.) If you go to a sale without this feature, ask the nearest bid spotter, if you lose track of bidding.

■ **Stick to your limit.** In the heat of the moment, this can be easier said than done. But I go to enough sales to know this: If you miss out on a particular horse, there will always be another one. Ultimately, though, you'll have to decide for yourself whether a certain horse is worth going over your budget.

Do NOT let your friends or family talk you into overspending on a horse. Let them know (beforehand) that you've done your research and have a cap on what you're willing to pay.

■ **Know the rules.** When you do buy at a sale, title and responsibility pass to you, the buyer, as soon as the horse leaves the sales ring and the purchase agreement is signed. (An auction employee will bring it to you.) Once you sign that paper, it's your responsibility to care for the horse, and to get him home. Most sales have insurance agents on hand, should you choose to insure him. And you'll usually find professional haulers standing by, if you need one. (Check this out with the sale company beforehand, if you don't have your own trailer.) Then get him home, and enjoy.

Doug Carpenter

Doug has been a professional horseman for the last 30 years. He started out as an apprentice trainer to Jack Farrell in Connecticut, eventually developing his own training business with Western pleasure as his specialty.

His list of AQHA World and Congress champions is lengthy, and includes Miss Docs Melody, TNT Fluid Fred, Racy Rumours, The Virginia Gent, and others. Doug has also made a name for himself in reining circles.

He and Bob have worked together to buy and sell horses over the years. Doug's eye for potential champions has earned him a large clientele that turn to him for expertise in horse buying. He's been so successful at buying and selling that he phased out training for the public to concentrate on sales for a variety of performance disciplines.

Examples of horses he and Bob have bought and sold reads like a who's who in the performance world: Boomernic, an NRHA Champion; Bueno Chexinic; Smart Zanolena, an NRCHA Champion; Chics Magic Potion, an NRCHA Champion; and Light N Fine, whose titles include the World's Greatest Horseman Championship with Bob.

Doug works out of his Doug Carpenter Livestock, in Sulphur, Oklahoma. Lately, the horseman has branched out beyond equine sales, and is also buying and selling bucking bulls.

Before you arrange to go see a horse, contact the owner/seller via phone and/or email, and ask a lot of questions to determine the horse's suitability for you. Our Smart Buyer Questionnaire will give you a good start.

CHAPTER 11

Smart Buyer
Questionnaire

Use these questions to gather preliminary information
and help weed out horses not suitable for your needs.
Then take the questionnaire with you when you try
a horse, so you can note what you observe.

"Don't be afraid of sounding ignorant or pushy. Most sellers won't
object to questions that are asked politely and respectfully. If a seller
does object, or gets murky with an answer, that's a red flag. An honest
seller knows the more information you gather up front, the less likely
you'll be to waste his or her time by looking at a horse that's not
suitable for you. And be sure to call those references!"

11

Bob's Personal Experience

Seller Info

Name: _____ Location/address: _____

_____

Phone numbers / Home: _____ Office: _____ Cell: _____

Website: _____

Horse Info

Name: _____ Breed: _____ Age: _____

Color/markings: _____ Height: _____

Registered name: _____

Registration number (verify w/assoc.; if/when you see the horse in person, verify that his
color/markings match his papers): _____

Sire/dam/bloodlines: _____

Show record? _____ What events? _____

Points earned (verify w/assoc.): _____

Health history? Has this horse ever (and if so, when):

Colicked? _____ Foundered? _____ Been sick/injured (explain)? _____

_____

Had surgery? _____ Had allergies/skin problems? _____

Has he been on medication? _____ If so, what? _____

Is he on medication now? _____ If so, what? _____

Been lame? _____ If so, explain: _____

Been denerved? _____

Needed corrective trimming/shoeing (and for what)? _____

When was he shod last? _____

When was he last dewormed (get details)? _____

When was he last vaccinated (get details)? _____

When did he last have his teeth floated (filed)? _____

Trainer's names/numbers, for references? _____

Temperament, on a scale of 1 to 10 (with 1 being the quietest): _____

Does this horse:

Load in a trailer? _____ Longe? _____ Tie/cross-tie? _____ Clip? _____

Bathe? _____ Stand for farrier/vet? _____ Stall? _____

Allow himself to be caught in pasture? _____

Is he good alone, in barn/pasture/when ridden? _____

Is he good with other horses? _____ Any saddling/bridling issues? _____

Crib? _____ Weave? _____ Wood chew? _____ Bite? _____

Pull back when tied? _____ Kick at people/horses? _____

Paw? _____ Stall kick? _____

Spook/shy? _____ Buck? _____ Rear? _____

Training history? Get specifics *you* want, such as how much riding has he had. If green, does he know leads? Neck reins? Lateral movement? Is he spur-stop trained (taught to slow/stop in response to leg pressure; a negative to many)? Lead changes? _____

_____

Mileage (for instance, has he been hauled extensively to different shows, arenas, trails, etc.): ___

What level of rider does he need? _____

Does he need lots of riding? Or can you ride once a week, if he's been turned out? _____

What's he doing currently? _____

When was he last hauled/shown? _____

What are horse's positives? _____

What are horse's negatives? _____

How long have you owned? _____ Reason for selling? _____

Do you allow a trial period? _____

Would you help me through a transition period? (A big RED FLAG if the seller waffles; he may be hiding or withholding something.) _____

A horse that's willing and responsive, and that can perform to the level at which you'll be riding and/or competing—while also giving you confidence—gets a BIG thumbs up.

CHAPTER 12

Smart Buyer
Test-Ride Guide

**Use this list of tips to
evaluate horses you go try.**

"One of the biggest things I see prospective buyers fall for is slick salesmanship. You drive up and the seller (or horse dealer) comes out with a horse that's shiny, clipped, trimmed, and dressed in fancy tack. You—or your kid—instantly fall in love with the horse. And he could be totally inappropriate for your needs.

Through experience I've learned that if you're looking for a horse for your child or novice significant other, leave that person at home. He or she may get emotionally attached to a horse that isn't suitable. Instead, prescreen your prospects, taking him or her to look at only horses that have passed your screening process.

When you screen, look past those first impressions, past the slick presentation, past all the bling on the saddle. Instead, use what you've learned in this book, and what you'll learn in this chapter, to really *test* this horse's suitability for you and/or your family. This is where a reputable trainer or agent can really help. They've seen all the sales tricks. Their focus will be on matching you with the right horse."

Y**ou've done all the legwork you can via email and phone calls.** And you've determined a certain horse deserves an in-person look. Here's how to be a smart shopper:

Step 1: Show up early

Plan to arrive *at least* 10 minutes early. (Earlier is better.) Hopefully you'll catch the seller getting the horse ready to show you. Look for signs the horse was worked before you got there, such as sweat marks. They may be a clue he's hotter or more energetic than he seems.

An early arrival may also give you a chance to study the horse in his living environment, giving you clues as to his attitude and potential vices.

Step 2: Take a good look

Ask to see the horse without a saddle at first, so you can evaluate his overall look and conformation, plus get some insights into his attitude. Look for...

- **Eye appeal (and attitude):** Get a first look at the horse in his stall, paddock, or in the cross-ties, while chatting with the seller.

 Thumbs up:

- He's attractive or appealing to look at, with a big, soft, kind eye and a relaxed expression. Don't turn your back on a plain-looking horse, as long as he's built like an athlete. By that, I mean he's balanced, with a long, well-shaped neck, long, sloping shoulder, short back, strong hip, and straight legs. If you're looking for a horse that'll be shown in judged events, or for re-sale, give him mental bonus points if he's oh-wow pretty. Pretty sells, both to judges and prospective buyers.

- He's not acting like an orangutan. Look for a subdued, respectful horse. However, personally, I won't walk away from one that jumps away from grooming or saddle pressure when being prepped for the test ride, which could indicate he'll have a lot of "feel" (responsiveness) to rein and leg cues. This, however, would be a thumbs down for a companion, family, kid's, or even many amateur horses.

A horse that stands quietly in the cross-ties, and greets you with polite, ears-up interest, gets a thumbs up.

This is balance: If you were to divide this horse's body into three parts (head and neck, shoulder to flank, and from the flank back), they mirror each other proportionally. He has a beautiful head that blends into a well-shaped neck. That, in turn, flows into a long, well-sloped shoulder, which blends into a strong back and a long, powerful hip (which matches the length and angle of his shoulder). His hocks are low to the ground and directly beneath the point of his hip, rather than positioned out behind him. He looks like an athlete.

 Thumbs down:

- Your first impression is that he looks as though he's made from spare parts, which indicates a lack of balance. Not only will he likely lack athleticism, if you're looking for a show horse, he'll not catch a judge's eye.

- He has a small, hard eye. In my experience, such horses can be tough minded.

- He looks as though he's about to come uncorked, standing or moving with his head up in the air, puffed up like a Macy's Parade balloon. *Note:* One possible exception would be if you're an experienced rider looking for a young horse. But while it's normal for a young horse to feel good, especially if he hasn't been worked, take a mental note of those signs. They could indicate a horse that's so hot he won't be cool for you.

Thumbs down: a small, hard eye.

■ **Conformation:** Ask the seller to hold the horse while you evaluate him from both sides, then front and back.

 Thumbs up:

• The horse's body blends seamlessly from one part to the next, indicating balance. (See photo, page 97.) Part of what makes a horse attractive is that kind of balance, which is an indicator of athleticism. Regardless of what you do with a horse, athleticism is a good thing. An unbalanced horse will find it difficult to do any task you ask him to, which can lead to resentment and resistance, as well as unsoundness. (Plus, he'll be NO fun to ride.)

Good muscle definition, and spread and width in the chest are also indicators of athleticism, as are straight, correct legs with good bone (of a width that appears proportional to his body—not too fine, not too coarse).

• He has a nice head that ties smoothly into a long, clean neck that comes out of the withers nearly level. (A neck that ties in high can mean a high-headed horse; those aren't much fun to ride, either!)

• The shoulder should be long and sloping, rather than short and/or straight up and down (which limits front-leg reach/athleticism, and can mean a jarring ride). This translates into freedom of movement there and in the front legs.

• That slope and length are mirrored in his hip, which translates directly into power.

• He's slightly higher in his withers than in his hip, meaning he'll naturally be able to shift his weight rearward and leave his shoulders freer for any maneuver you ask, whether its curling around a barrel in speed events, walking over a downed tree on the trail, or sitting over his hocks and "walking" with his front legs through a dynamic sliding stop. *Note:* If you're shopping for youngsters, growth spurts may cause the hip to be higher than the withers. This is where an experienced trainer/agent can help you determine how the horse will mature.

• He has reasonably prominent withers, which tie into a short back (a long back indicates weakness).

• He "V's up" well from the chest, indicating good muscle definition. He has good spread and width through his chest.

Leg faults I can (and can't) live with

I look at a horse's legs from a trainer's standpoint, not a veterinarian's. Based on years of experience, I've learned what faults seem to lead to unsoundness in my program, and what don't. While there will always be individual exceptions, these are my general rules of thumb on some common conformation flaws:

- **Club foot** (a straighter-than-normal foot axis, caused by a flexor tendon contracture): Unless it's really mild, I'll pass; I've had problems keeping such horses sound.

- **Pigeon toes** (horse toes in): Pass. I find that these horses may not stay sound at my level of work.

- **Toes out:** I'll usually accept such a horse if the fault is slight, because generally he'll stay sound. (I'll pass on a horse that's straight from forearm to ankle, then really toes out from there down.)

- **Over at the knees:** I don't mind a horse being over at the knees; you see a lot of hunters like this. They seem to take the concussion better than a horse that's calf-kneed (see below).

- **Calf-kneed** (back at the knees): Pass; this fault places more concussion on the joint than normal or "over-at-the" knees.

- **Post-legged:** I'll pass on a horse with straight up-and-down hind legs; such conformation minimizes shock absorption, increasing joint concussion.

(*Note:* If I get a horse with less-than-perfect legs, I'll leave him alone, shoeing-wise. By the time he arrives at my place, he's usually a late yearling or older. The time for corrective shoeing is past. At that point, it'd likely do more harm than good.)

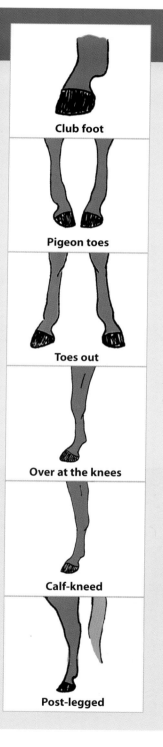

Club foot

Pigeon toes

Toes out

Over at the knees

Calf-kneed

Post-legged

- His front legs are straight and correct, with short cannon bones and good bone. His pasterns slope at an angle similar to his shoulder, and are long enough to act as shock absorbers, but not so long as to be weak. (For information on common leg faults, see "Leg Faults I Can—And Can't—Live With," on page 99.)

- He's well muscled through his hips, buttocks, and gaskins, and his hocks are low to the ground. When viewed from behind, his lower hind legs come straight down from his hocks, so he neither toes in nor out. This means he's built to be sound—and athletic.

 Thumbs down

- He lacks balance. His neck is too short (hindering balance and athleticism). His back is too long (meaning weak). And/or his hip is too short (adversely affecting power and balance).

This horse shows good muscling in his hips, butt, and gaskins (the top part of his hind legs, just above his hocks). His lower legs (which you can just see through his tail) come straight down from his hocks, which can be a good indicator of future soundness.

- He's naturally high-headed. He stands with his head and neck up in the air like a giraffe (which will put them uncomfortably close to your face when you ride!), rather than having them come out nearly level from his withers.

- He's a mature horse that's higher in his hip than at his withers. Such a horse will have trouble rocking his weight rearward, which will negatively impact his athleticism. (See photo at left.) It may also make him more prone to soundness issues on his front end, since his weight will be "dumped" there.

Compare this horse with the one on page 97—she's as unbalanced as he is balanced. She looks like three different horses pieced together! Her neck ties low into her chest and has no definition. The fact that it's heavy on the underside means she's going to be naturally high-headed. She has a short, straight shoulder and a long back, plus a hip that lacks the slope or length needed for power. Even if she's good minded, she'll naturally have a harder time doing anything athletic than the previous horse. She's not built for it.

- He's too massive in the chest, which can make it harder for him (or any horse) to cross over in front for events such as reining, than it is for a slighter-built horse. His bulk gets in his way. *Note:* If I like the horse, and he has a good, trainable mind (which we'll test in a minute), I won't disqualify him for this. Trainability can overcome some faults. This is one of them.

- He's narrow-chested, limiting his lung capacity and making his front legs look as though they both originate from the same "hole." His cannon bones are long and spindly, rather than short and strong. And his pasterns are short and straight up and down (which will result in excess concussion in his front feet, and a jarring stride), or excessively long and sloping (meaning weak), rather than sloped at an angle that roughly matches his shoulder.

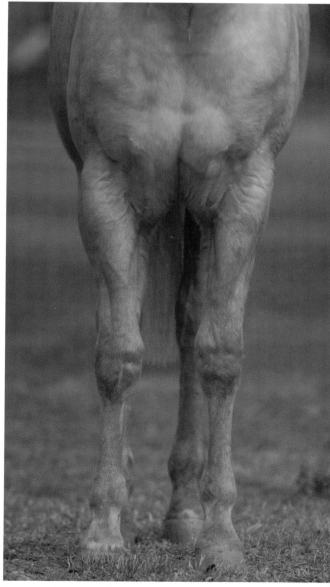

- He toes in, toes out, or has any of the other conformation faults I talk about in the box on page 99. And/or, he has an obvious blemish or problem that could interfere with performance (if you seek a riding horse). For more information on such problems, see Chapter 14: "The Prepurchase Exam."

- He's narrow through his hind end, and lacks adequate muscling, which makes him look weak (because he *is* weak!).

- His hocks are set high off the ground, rather than low. Such hind-end conformation can torch power and athleticism. And/or, he toes out (cow-hocked) or toes in behind.

- He shows signs of inadequate care that could lead to later lameness or health issues. These include poor or inadequate shoeing (long toes, chipped, cracking hooves, loose shoes), untended wounds, poor coat, dull eye.

If you're not happy with what you see here, thank the seller and move on. If you like what you see, move on with your "test." Don't be shy. You're the one who'll be writing the check.

The mare's narrow chest and lack of well-defined muscling further contribute to an overall lack of potential athleticism.

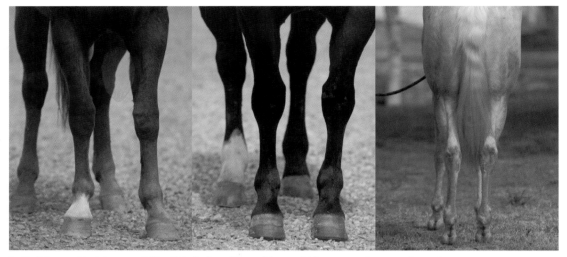

Left: A horse that toes out like this below the ankle could be prone to soundness issues. **Center:** Correct legs, which are straight from point of shoulder, through knee, ankle, and front of hoof, bode best for future soundness. **Right:** A narrow hind end that lacks muscling (in a mature horse) can indicate a lack of strength and athleticism.

Step 3: Test his suitability

I'll break this down into the same categories we used in Chapter 2: "Meet Your Match."

■ A. Companion horse

Note: These will form the basic test for any type of horse you buy, regardless of whether he's a backyard companion or national-level show horse.

The ground-test components:

Ask to see the horse in a stall, if he'll be stalled at your facility. (This can be particularly insightful at feed time, so time your visit or the stall "experiment" accordingly. Stall aggression, kicking, and other vices often show up then.)

Thumbs up: He's quiet and relaxed in a stall setting. He doesn't exhibit signs of any stall vices (see Chapter 8).

Thumbs down: He's restless, and/or shows signs of having stall vices.

Ask to see the horse caught in a large paddock or pasture setting.

Thumbs up: He can be easily caught.

Thumbs down: He plays hard to get. (If you really like him otherwise, you can ask the seller to work on the problem, then schedule a time to come back and see the horse.)

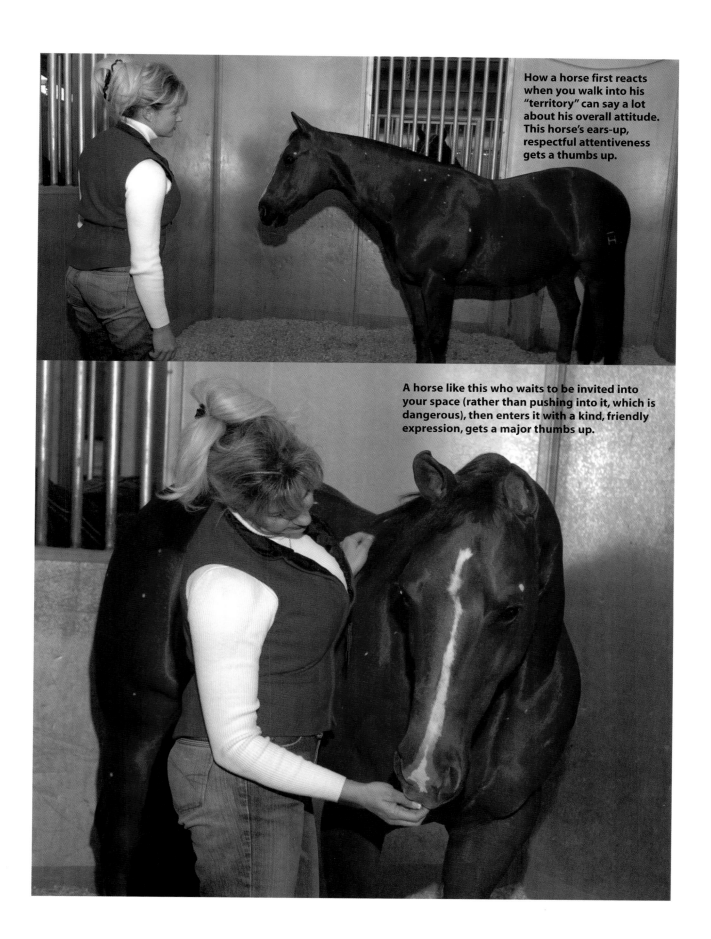

How a horse first reacts when you walk into his "territory" can say a lot about his overall attitude. This horse's ears-up, respectful attentiveness gets a thumbs up.

A horse like this who waits to be invited into your space (rather than pushing into it, which is dangerous), then enters it with a kind, friendly expression, gets a major thumbs up.

Observe the horse as you approach in the paddock (or initially in his stall).

👍 *Thumbs up:* He turns and looks at you with his ears up, which tells you he's attentive and respectful. *Smart buyer tip:* Gently push his nose away. He gets bonus points if he yields to that pressure easily and takes a step or two back, meaning he's respectful.

Top: If the horse will be living in a paddock with other horses, ask to see him in that setting, and observe his behavior. Does he handle being around other horses well? Or is he aggressive, chasing them, and/or biting and kicking? If it's the latter, and unless you can house him alone, I'd pass. After you've watched him, be sure to see if he can be caught! **Bottom:** A horse that turns his tail toward you when you approach, as this horse is, and/or pins his ears, gets a BIG thumbs down. Pass!

👎 *Thumbs down:*
- He pins his ears and wrings his tail when you simply look at him. Worse still, he turns his tail, or otherwise acts threatening.

- He crowds or steps into your space, which shows a lack of respect (and is downright dangerous).

- He makes you feel nervous in his company in any way, at any point in your ground test. That's not companionship! Keep looking. There are plenty of nice horses out there.

Observe the horse being led.

👍 *Thumbs up:* He walks alongside willingly (and quietly), easily guiding in any direction, and stopping/starting with minimal halter pressure.

👎 *Thumbs down:* He charges ahead, drags behind, jigs with excitement, swishes his tail, or tries to push into his handler with his nose or head. (This is especially key for a child's or novice horse.)

Ask to see the horse tied in a variety of locations, such as the barn aisle, arena fence post, and trailer.

👍 *Thumbs up:* He stands relaxed and quiet, exerting no pressure against the restraint.

👎 *Thumbs down:* He moves restlessly, swishes his tail (a sign of impatience and irritation), paws, and/or tries to pull back and break free.

Top: A horse that walks alongside you or his handler quietly and willingly while being led, stopping, starting, and guiding with minimal halter pressure as this horse is—and staying out of your space—gets a thumbs up. **Bottom:** If he drags behind like this horse, charges ahead, or butts into you (a major sign of disrespect and one of my pet peeves), thumbs down!

Ask to see the horse in a turnout situation, if he'll be housed in a paddock, or turned out, at your place. If he'll be turned out alone, ask to have his buddies moved away from him.

 Thumbs up: He quietly sniffs around, then goes to grazing or exploring his space.

Thumbs down:

- He paces the fence in his enclosure, a sign of restlessness and insecurity.

- He screams for his friends, another sign of insecurity (and a noise that gets old fast).

The test-ride components: N/A

■ **B. Companion horse you can ride lightly**

The ground-test components:
Go through all the tests outlined in "A," above. Add the following:

Ask to observe the horse being saddled and bridled.

Thumbs up: The horse quietly stands while the seller tacks him up.

Thumbs down: He resents being saddled (won't stand still; swishes tail in irritation) and/or resists/refuses to be bridled.

The test-ride components:
(Ask the seller to ride the horse first, so you can see if he's anything you truly want to ride.)

Observe the horse being mounted.

Thumbs up: He stands quietly, not moving off until the rider asks him to.

Thumbs down: He won't stand quietly (a sign that he has huge gaps in his training—and also a dangerous situation for you).

If the horse will be turned out alone at your place, ask to see him turned out alone when you try him. If he paces or runs the fence in a show of anxiety, he may be insecure (not a fun horse to have), or too darn hot to be cool.

Ask to watch the horse at all three gaits, plus stopping and turning. Also ask to see him ridden inside and outside an enclosed area, such as an arena.

 Thumbs up:

- He willingly moves forward, stops, and turns with his topline level, his tail and mouth quiet.

- The horse is nimble on his feet—he's not stumbling around and getting in his own way.

- His demeanor doesn't change whether he's ridden inside an arena, or outside it.

- He shows no signs of being ring- or gate-sour, meaning he doesn't try to dart out the gate whenever he goes by, and/or doesn't hesitate to walk into the arena.

- He looks like a horse that would be fun to ride.

 Thumbs down:

- He lacks basic go, stop, and turn skills; he's hot/nervous to ride, jigging and pulling against the bit.

- He regularly pins his ears and wrings his tail, indicating a negative attitude toward his rider.

Test tips

When looking for a prospect or broke horse in a specific event, be sure to test the horse's aptitude. For instance, if you're looking for a cutting, cow, or roping horse, be sure to work the horse on cattle (or ask to see him worked on cattle).

If you're looking for a hunter, ask to see the horse jumped, even if it's free-jumped.

Don't be shy. Some horses that are bred to work cattle or jump lack the mental or physical ability to do so. It's better to find that out *before* you write the check. (And if you lack the experience to know exactly what to look for in a "specialty" horse, be sure to hire an experienced agent to help you.)

A horse that moves forward, guides, and stops quietly and willingly and in response to light rein and leg aids gets a major thumbs up. Ask to see the seller (or your trainer/agent) ride him first, in case he's not a horse you'd want to ride (or own).

- He's resistant to pressure on his nose or in his mouth (exhibited by bracing his neck and/or tossing his head), or to leg pressure (such as bracing against the rider's leg, or kicking at it).

- He trips frequently or otherwise appears to lack athleticism.

- He's "looky" or spooky. (If he's this way in his home environment, he'll only get worse when you ride him in a new environment.)

Ask the seller to ride the horse away from the barn and his buddies, to see how he handles being ridden alone.

 Thumbs up: His willingness and demeanor don't change.

Thumbs down:
- He's reluctant or refuses to leave his buddies or barn, and/or acts desperate to get back to them.

- He suddenly acts green broke and/or young, and you lack the skills and time to work with him, or the money to have him trained. (See Chapter 6, "When Green Means No," page 45.)

If you still like him, ask to ride the horse.

 Thumbs up: He's light and responsive to your leg and rein cues, willingly moving forward, speeding up, slowing down, and stopping inside and outside an enclosed area.

Thumbs down: He's dull and resistant (meaning his first response to any question

A horse that's resistant and/or hot and chargey when being ridden, or that makes you feel insecure (or just plain afraid) in any way, gets a giant thumbs down. There are plenty of other (and better) horses out there.

you ask is "NO!"), or hot, chargey, and/or spooky, meaning he has an energy level that would require being worked 6 days a week to keep him quiet. (This is especially key if you only have time to ride occasionally.) Or…he makes you feel less than secure and confident on his back, in any way. Riding is supposed to be fun!

■ C. Companion horse you can haul out for long trail rides

The ground-test components:
Go through the tests outlined in "B," above. Add the following:

Ask to see the horse loaded and unloaded in a trailer. (*Tip:* Also ask the seller to haul him around the block, to see how he rides when moving. He gets a thumbs up if he's quiet.)

 Thumbs up: He walks right onto and off of the trailer with confidence, standing quietly while in the trailer.

 Thumbs down: He's reluctant or refuses to load. (That would make it tough to haul out to a trail!) If you *really* like the horse after the test, ask the seller to work on his loading skills, and arrange another "test" visit.

The test-ride components:
Go through the tests outlined in "B," above. Add the following:

Arrange for the seller to haul the horse to a group ride, so you can observe the horse's attitude in a new area, and within a group of horses, plus test his trail skills.

 Thumbs up:
- He handles being hauled to a new place calmly. The horse willingly motors along anywhere in the group, whether he's the first horse, the last horse, or somewhere in the middle.

- He willingly negotiates ditches, logs, water, and other obstacles.

 Thumbs down:
- He's amped and anxious in a new environment, requiring a long period of longeing before he settles down.

Be sure to ask to see the horse being loaded and unloaded (after all, you've got to get him home!). If he resists or refuses being loaded, as this horse is here, that's a thumbs down. But if you *really* like everything else about the horse, ask the seller to work on the horse's loading skills, then arrange for another test.

If the horse is spooky like this at home or in a new setting, especially if he's been advertised as "broke," well, you know the drill by now. Thumbs down!!

- He's aggressive toward other horses, threatening to bite and/or kick. Red flag! He could hurt another horse, or a rider.

- He won't quietly follow other horses, insisting instead on surging to the front. That gets old fast on what's supposed to be a relaxing ride.

- He spooks constantly, and refuses to go near such common obstacles as water.

- You aren't allowed to test ride in a group or on the trail. Red flag! The seller's hoping you get this horse home before discovering his "holes."

■ D. All of the above, plus a horse you can go to clinics with

The ground-test components:
Go through the tests outlined in "C," above.

The test-ride components:
Go through the tests outlined in "C," above. Look for an ears-up, happy, relaxed attitude, and willingness to work that signifies a good work ethic and an aptitude for learning.

■ E. All of the above, plus a horse you can show at the open or club level

The ground-test components:
Go through the tests outlined in "D," above.

The test-ride components:
Go through the tests outlined in "D," above. Add the following:

Ask the seller to demonstrate the horse's event-specific skills (in those events in which you wish to show).

A horse with a naturally level topline like this one, and flat-kneed, sweepy, and naturally cadenced movement, will impress judges in judged events—and sellers if you decide to sell him at some point. He'll also be more comfortable to ride than a horse with jerky, short-strided movement.

 Thumbs up:

- The horse willingly performs those skills in a manner suitable to be competitive at your desired level of showing.

- For judged events: The horse is a good mover. He has the flat-kneed, sweepy stride of an athlete, and moves with a naturally level topline (all of which will be rewarded at any level of showing).

 Thumbs down:

- He shows any signs of resistance and/or fear when asked to perform. These include pinned ears, swishing tail, raised head, braced jaw, and general nervousness.

- He moves with a choppy, knee-high stride (unless he's of a breed specifically bred for it).

Arrange with the seller to watch the horse being shown. This is KEY: Many horses perform beautifully at home, but fall apart, or show signs of burn out, in a show environment.

Thumbs up: The horse is as reliable at a horse show as he is at home, willingly performing the maneuvers asked of him with minimal up-front prep.

Thumbs down:

- He requires long sessions on the longe line before you ride him at a show. Such a horse will be time-intensive and far less fun than one that's broke, safe, and ready to show.

- He shows any signs of being show sour. That is, the horse pins his ears, wrings his tail, and acts sour (or misbehaves) in the show pen.

- The seller tells you he can't take him to a show for any reason. That's a red flag, especially for a show horse.

- The horse isn't being consistently shown at the level at which you desire to show. This could be a sign that he has problems in the show pen, or problems outside it (such as behavior or lameness issues) that preclude him from performing.

■ **F. A horse you can keep at home and show competitively at a local level without regular professional help**

The ground-test components:
Go through the tests outlined in "E," above.

The test-ride components:
Go through the tests outlined in "E," above. Add the following:

If you like the horse, ask the trainer or trainers you'll be using on occasion to look at him, to verify his suitability for you and your competitive goals.

 Thumbs up: They agree with you and like the horse.

 Thumbs down: They don't. That could be a clear sign that your emotions have taken over, clouding reality. Listen to them. If you have to try to talk them into a horse, that's a major red flag.

■ **G. A do-it-yourself show horse that you can take lessons on once or twice a week, to ratchet up your competitive edge**

"Yes sir, you'll love him, trust me— everything I've told you is true (not!)."

If you're buying a cow horse and/or roper, ask to see him worked on cattle. (With a roper, above right, be sure to see how he behaves in the box.) Same with a trail horse, barrel racer, hunter/jumper, or any other event you're specifically shopping for. Otherwise, how will you know if he has the aptitude for the job?

The test-ride components:

Go through the tests outlined in "F," above. *Note:* With regular professional help, you may be able to begin with a younger, greener horse (say, younger than 5 or 6 for a stock horse, or 7 or 8 for a hunter/jumper/dressage horse). Ask the trainer or trainers you'll be working with to help you evaluate the horse's ability and aptitude for a more advanced level of learning, athleticism, and performance ability than has been outlined in the previous scenarios.

■ H. A horse to be kept in full-time training

The ground-test components:

Go through the tests outlined in "G," above (that are applicable). *Note:* Your trainer should be involved in any purchase, since he or she will be working with the horse and you. He or she may see promise in a younger and/or less-experienced horse that might not suit a do-it-yourself buyer.

The test-ride components:

Go through the tests outlined in "G," above. Add the following:

Ask the seller to demonstrate any maneuvers specific to your specialty.

 Thumbs up: You and your trainer agree the horse has the aptitude to help you reach your goals. You click with the horse, and enjoy working with him. Your trainer clicks with the horse.

Thumbs down:
- The horse lacks the aptitude, or attitude, to do the job for which you're buying him.

When shopping for a horse that'll be in full-time training, your trainer should be very involved in the search. If, after the test ride, he or she gives the horse a thumbs down, keep looking. You'll all be happier (including your eventual horse) if your trainer likes him. If you don't trust your trainer's opinion, you're with the wrong trainer.

Photo by Darrell Dodds

If you're looking at a show horse, ask to see him at a show. Some horses are the picture of perfection at home, but fall apart in the show ring. If you want to show, that would be a big (you guessed it) thumbs down.

• You don't click with him. Even if you'll have the horse in full-time training, you still have to feel good about writing the checks. If you don't like him, don't let your trainer talk you into him.

• Your trainer doesn't like the horse. It won't be any fun for you—or your horse—if your trainer has negative feelings about him.

■ **I. A national-level horse to be in full-time training**

Go through the tests outlined in "H," above. Your trainer will help you select a horse that matches your goals and ability, and has the potential to reach a higher level of performance than any others discussed so far in this chapter.

■ **J. World-class competitor**

At this level, your trainer will be involved every step of the way. Allow him or her to guide you through the test ride, but don't hesitate to speak up if you don't feel comfortable with the horse for any reason. It's your money (and your fun).

■ **K. Investment buy**

Go through the "ground" and "test ride" tests outlined above. Watch for the following thumbs down, and discuss them with a trainer/agent.

 Potential thumbs down:

• The horse isn't amateur-friendly. Unless you're a pro selling to fellow pros, amateurs will be your biggest market. The broker and safer a horse is, the easier he is to sell.

• He's a horse that you don't like and wouldn't be willing to keep the rest of his life. That's because something could happen that could cause him to live out his days with you (such as a catastrophic injury). And, if you dislike him that much, chances are other people will, too. That means you may not be able to sell him.

Additional
test-ride tips

■ **Be courteous to the seller**—it's his horse you're trying.

■ **Try the horse for a reasonable amount of time.** It shouldn't take half a day to figure out if he'll work.

■ **Stick to what the horse knows,** unless you have approval from the owner. For instance, you want to test a hunter prospect over a low jump to evaluate his attitude and form, but you shouldn't try to rope off him.

■ **Don't over-do it.** I have people who come to my place and want to run and slide-stop sale horses too much. That's hard on the horse…and the seller.

A horse that balks when asked to leave the barn or his buddies is showing signs of insecurity, which can be tough to overcome. My recommendation? Walk away and keep shopping.

CHAPTER 13

7 Signs You Should Walk Away

Keep your eyes peeled when you first look at a horse (and the seller). There may be clear signs that you should "pass" on this one.

"I can't tell you how many times I've gone to look at a horse and found him or her to be cranky, rude, balky, and/or generally disrespectful. If it's a mare, the seller inevitably says, 'I don't know what's wrong with her today. She must be in season.' Well I don't want a horse that's a witch when in season! If the horse is a gelding or stallion, he must be having a 'bad day.'

That's two fatal strikes against a sale. First, when I see a horse with a 'tude, regardless of how pretty or talented he is, I'm out of there. Attitude in a horse is everything, just as it is in people. I can overlook a lot, but I can't overlook that.

Second, when a seller starts to make excuses for a horse's behavior, I'm done. 'In season?', 'Bad day?' And my favorite, 'He's never done that!' Don't believe any of them. Which means you can't believe anything else the seller says, either.

Note: A few of these red flags (or thumbs down) I've covered elsewhere in the book. To me, they bear repeating."

You've heard of gut feelings, right? I can tell you that when I first get out of my car at a barn, meet the seller, and see the horse, my gut is working overtime. I'm processing everything I'm seeing, wondering whether I should go through with the shopping exercise, or make a polite excuse to head home.

Believe me, I've made plenty of polite excuses. And you should, too, if you see any of the following signs, which can indicate the horse won't be much fun to work or live with. (These are in addition, of course, to the obvious signs such as biting, kicking, bucking, spooking, bolting, rearing, etc.)

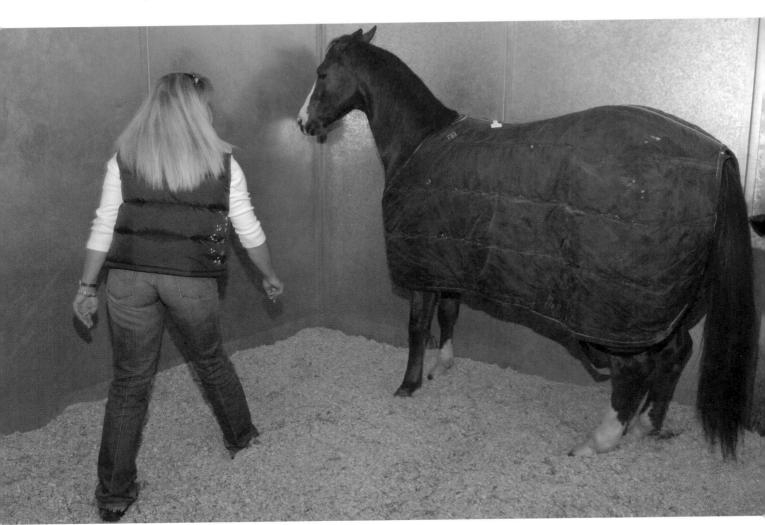

Is he rude? Aggressive? Or just territorial in his stall? Regardless, he doesn't look like fun to be around, and could be dangerous to you and to others. Unless you're a highly experienced handler and he's some kind of freaky talent, I'd suggest you walk away. There are too many nice horses out there.

Sign #1: Bad attitude, horse

(For more information on these attitudes, see "Chapter 8: Vice Squad," page 61.)

- **Cranky.** When you approach him in the crossties, stall, or pasture, he pins his ears and swishes his tail in annoyance. And/or, he shakes his head and wrinkles his nose/lips at you, which is threatening behavior.

- **Rude.** The horse turns tail when you approach him in his stall or pasture, pointing his kicking gear in your general direction.

- **Impatient.** When tied or standing in his stall, the horse paws repeatedly, and moves restlessly.

- **Kicks.** He lifts a hind leg, threatening to kick when you approach. (If he actually kicks, you'd hear my tires squealing as I bailed out of there!)

- **Cinchy.** He snakes his head around to bite, swishes his tail, and/or attempts to kick when being saddled up for your test ride. (Be sure to watch him being readied for the ride. You can learn a lot about his attitude from doing so.)

Note: Some horses are territorial in their stall or space. They can be cranky there but fine outside or under saddle. It's up to you to decide if you think a particular horse is worth a further look if you spot a behavior such as pinned ears.

Sign #2: Herd/barn bound

- **Antsy.** When you or the horse's handler try to lead or ride him away from his equine buddies and/or the barn, the horse jigs (or worse) and calls to his buddies. The farther away he's taken, the worse he gets.

A horse that drags behind when being led (top photo) or tries to walk on top of you or bump you with his head (bottom photo) is showing signs of disrespect. It's been my experience that the same disrespect will show up when you ride, so when I see it on the ground, it's a red flag.

Disrespect on the ground is always a red flag to me.
The horse will very likely disrespect you
when you're on his back.

A cranky attitude when being handled on the ground can transfer into problems when ridden. If it's bad enough, you might want to walk away. At the very least, you'll need to decide whether you want to live with this kind of attitude in your barn.

■ **Balky.** Or…he gets balky when led and/or ridden away from his barn or buddies, constantly trying to stop and turn back. *Smart buyer's tip:* As a part of any test ride, be sure to take the horse away from his friends and the barn. If he starts misbehaving, you'll know he's barn or buddy sour, which can be a pain to deal with. Is it curable? Generally, with work. But are there other horses out there that don't suffer from this form of equine insecurity? You betcha.

Sign #3: Space invader

■ **Rude.** When you lead him, the horse walks into and over you. He may also drag behind or pull ahead. Any of these signs show a lack of training and respect. It's been my experience that both will show up when you go to ride the horse. That's why disrespect on the ground is always a red flag to me. The horse will very likely disrespect you when you're on his back.

■ **Butt-head.** He butts you with his head. No, this is not a "cute" sign of affection. Rather, it's a sign of disrespect. You can bet that horse wouldn't head butt the boss hoss in his herd. He'd know if he did, he'd get bitten or kicked. If he's head-butting you, he considers *himself* the boss hoss in your herd of two. That's not a good thing. And again, such an attitude can transfer to work under saddle.

A horse that's hotter or spookier (or shorter or older or anything else) than the seller represented in his ad or on the phone is a red flag. It means you can't trust anything else the seller says. Walk away!

Sign #4: Lame

■ **Breeding stock.** If the horse is intended as a companion animal or breeding stock (he won't be ridden), *and* a vet says he's serviceably sound for such a job (see Chapter 14, "The Prepurchase Exam"), you may want to consider him. But I'd only do so with a reputable veterinarian's okay.

■ **Riding stock.** Run. I mean it. If you go to test ride a horse and he's lame, I don't care what excuse the seller (See Sign #6) gives you. Leave.

Sign #5: Seller refuses a drug test

■ **You like the horse…**and ask if the seller would object to you having your veterinarian do a drug screen as part of a prepurchase exam. This is a great "honesty test." While drug screens can be expensive and can't uncover all behavior-modifying drugs (learn more about these in Chapter 14), the question is free and will tell you a lot about the seller. Someone without anything to hide will say, "Feel free." A seller with something to hide will hem and haw, or start making excuses. In such a case, walk away.

> The horse misbehaves or resists in any way… and the seller says, "He's never done that before." Guess what. He has.

Sign #6: Seller has too many excuses

■ **Disconnect.** The horse doesn't match the ad. He's older/younger, shorter/taller, greener, hotter, lame (see Sign #4) or generally different than he was represented. The seller has plenty of excuses. Don't listen to any of them.

■ **The horse misbehaves or resists in any way…**and the seller says, "He's never done that before." Guess what. He has.

■ **See above.** Check out the anecdote at the beginning of this chapter to discover more common seller excuses.

Sign #7: Bad attitude, seller

■ **Rude.** Just as I can't abide a rude, pushy, or disrespectful attitude in a horse, neither can I abide it in a seller. Feel free to shut down the shopping exercise if he or she makes you uncomfortable in any way. You're spending your time and potentially your money on this horse. The seller should put out the red carpet and treat you with respect and a professional attitude. Anything less isn't deserving of your time. Period.

■ **Fear.** Watch the seller's body language. Heads up if he or she acts afraid to handle or ride the horse, suggesting that you do so, instead. There's a reason he or she is afraid. And there's no reason for you to find out why—the hard way.

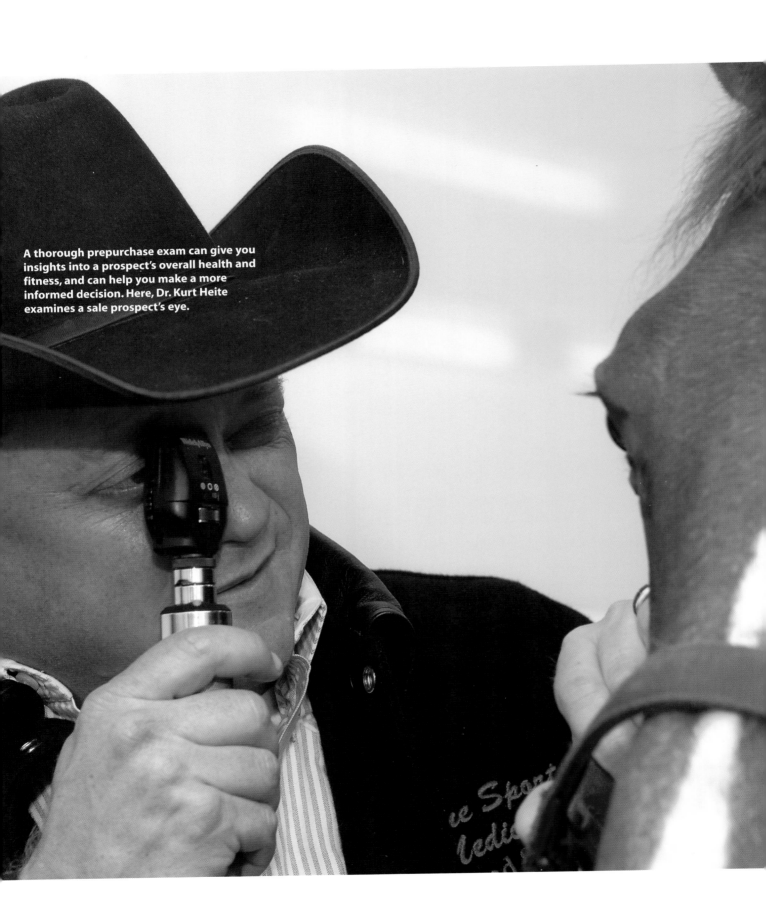

A thorough prepurchase exam can give you insights into a prospect's overall health and fitness, and can help you make a more informed decision. Here, Dr. Kurt Heite examines a sale prospect's eye.

CHAPTER 14

The Prepurchase Exam

Learn what "vetting" your horse can—
and can't—tell you, from top performance
horse veterinarian Kurt Heite, DVM.

14

Bob's Personal Experience

"I frequently hear of and see people back off of buying a horse because of a minor (and manageable) wear-and-tear condition that showed up during a prepurchase exam. A lot of people expect perfection. I'm here to tell you there's no such thing in a horse, or a human for that matter. Heck, if you vetted Michael Jordan when he was playing basketball, do you think he'd pass? I guarantee he wouldn't. I suggest you ask your prepurchase vet this question: If this was *your* money, and you wanted to do with this horse exactly as I want to do with him, would you buy him? The answer will tell you what you need to know."

I'm glad Bob asked me to talk to you about prepurchase exams (PPEs). While it's impossible to predict a horse's future health and soundness, you can hedge your bets by investing in a PPE, a head-to-toe veterinary examination designed to unearth existing (and some potential) problems that could adversely affect the horse's performance. By having your prospect "vetted" you'll get a reasonable idea of his health and soundness, which will help you decide whether or not to buy him.

In this chapter, I'll tell you what information a PPE will and won't provide, based on my years of performing thousands of them as an FEI-approved equine sports medicine veterinarian. I'll focus on the exam for a performance/riding horse. (Tests will vary for a young, untrained horse or breeding stock.) I'll share why you should invest in one, and what it'll cost. I'll also walk you through a standard exam, so you'll know what to expect, and what the vet will be looking for.

Then I'll explain what optional tests are available, should you choose to pursue more in-depth procedures. Finally, since it's a rare horse that doesn't have some problems, I'll tell you what conditions I, as a rider of performance horses, would consider living with, and some that would really concern me.

> By having your prospect "vetted" you'll get a reasonable idea of his health and soundness, which will help you decide whether or not to buy him.

Prepurchase fast facts

What it is: a report of veterinary findings on that horse on the day he's examined, based on a thorough prepurchase examination, plus any additional testing you and your vet feel is necessary.

What it isn't:
- **A guarantee of future soundness.**
- **An opinion on the horse's suitability** (beyond serviceable soundness) for your chosen event—that's a trainer's/agent's job. (For this chapter, I'll lump "trainer/agent" under the single term, "trainer.")
- **A pass/fail scenario.** Any decision based on exam discoveries will be yours and/or your trainer's.
- **An opinion on the horse's value.** It's your and/or your trainer's role to determine whether the horse is fairly priced.

Choosing the right prepurchase veterinarian

Choose a vet who specializes in what you want to do, and who does a lot of PPEs. For instance, if you're buying breeding stock, hire a vet who's a breeding expert.

If you're buying a performance horse, choose a veterinarian whose area of expertise is performance horses. (Because that is my area of expertise, I keep up with the latest in performance health technology. However, I don't keep up with breeding stuff; you do NOT want me to do a PPE on horses to be used specifically for breeding purposes! And you don't want a breeding expert to evaluate a horse's performance health and soundness.)

Here are some tips for finding a good prepurchase vet:

■ **Ask your trainer** and/or reputable trainers in your chosen event for their recommendations.

■ **Contact the American Association of Equine Practitioners,** and ask for a performance horse vet in your (or the seller's) area. Go to www.aaep.org or call 859-233-0147.

■ **Contact your regional equine veterinary school** and ask for recommendations.

■ **Opt for a vet with digital x-ray technology.** Such x-rays provide superior diagnostic capability over both hard (standard) film and fluoroscopy (a form of video x-ray). This is especially key if you're buying a horse for resale; *your* buyer may opt for digital images during a PPE, which could turn up something you missed if your vet didn't use them. Digital x-rays can also be instantly e-mailed or burned to a CD, for review for a second opinion.

■ **Pick a vet that can communicate on your level,** meaning one that you're comfortable talking to. You want him or her to be able to break down any findings into layman's terms. And, you especially want to be able to ask any and all questions that arise.

■ **Try to avoid using the seller's and/or horse's regular veterinarian,** if possible, to avoid a potential conflict-of-interest situation.

When you get the vet's input, make sure you understand it. The only stupid question is one you don't ask.

What it isn't (continued):

■ **A lameness exam for the seller at your expense.** If the horse turns out to be lame, and the cause is not easily diagnosed, let the seller handle the diagnosis and treatment. If you're still interested in the horse after that, you can schedule a repeat PPE.

Why you need it: A PPE is a money-saving expense. Sound contradictory? It's not. If the exam should uncover a problem that you and/or your trainer can't live with, such as something that could render the horse unsound for your purposes, you've saved your up-front investment, plus any subsequent funds you'd spend on feeding, housing, and caring for a horse you may not be able to use…or sell.

Who should be there:

■ **You (the buyer):** You have the most to gain, since you're paying for the exam, and ultimately, the horse. If the vet discovers something on his basic exam, you can immediately discuss it and determine whether or not to proceed with further testing. *Bonus:* If you've spent little time around the horse, you'll have a chance to see how he reacts to being handled from head to tail.

■ **The seller (or his or her trainer):** This person can provide the vet with the horse's background, such as deworming and vaccination history, plus incidence of colic, unsoundness, anhidrosis (inability to sweat), or other such problems. The seller may not disclose such problems, but any history will be helpful.

■ **Your trainer:** He or she can help you interpret findings, evaluate the horse's serviceability for your chosen event, and help you make the final yes-or-no decision. If you're a novice buyer and don't have a trainer, I'd agree with Bob and *strongly* suggest you hire a reputable one to help you evaluate the horse's suitability to you and your event, and to be present at the PPE. (See Chapter 3: "How (And Why) To Get Help From A Pro," page 19.)

What it'll cost: Plan on spending from around $300 to $1,500 for a PPE (rates may go up or down, depending on your area/veterinarian, and wants/needs). The lower figure is for the basic exam outlined on the next page. The higher figure includes additional diagnostic tests, such as radiographs (x-rays), drug screens, ultrasounds, and the like, which I'll talk about as well.

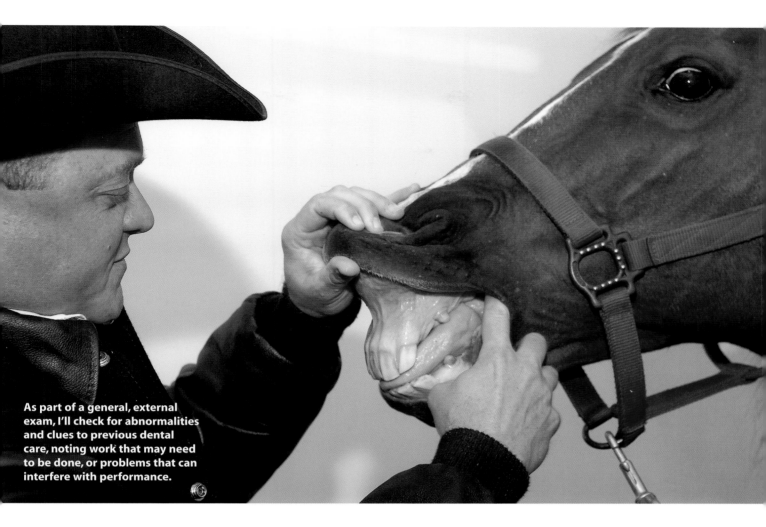

As part of a general, external exam, I'll check for abnormalities and clues to previous dental care, noting work that may need to be done, or problems that can interfere with performance.

The exam

Note: Medical conditions in **bold** are explained in the "Can you live with it?" chart on page 138, along with some other commonly found conditions.

1. Description. I'll start by noting on a checklist-type form the horse's name, breed, age, and sex. I'll then write down his color, any brands or markings, and his intended use.

2. General external systems. I'll then check the following:

- **Conformation:** I'll note any obvious conformation flaws that could impact soundness/ performance.
- **Temperature:** I'll take and record the horse's temperature.
- **Body condition:** I'll observe his general condition—is he underweight, overweight, or just right?
- **Mouth:** I'll check for abnormalities and clues to previous dental care. If the teeth need floating (filing) I'll note it for the new owner. I'll also note anything that could interfere with performance, such as specific dental problems or a tongue laceration.
- **Ears:** I'll look for signs of abnormal growths, or for infection or infestation, such as from ticks or mites.

Bob's advice

Here's my two cents, based on the hundreds (or more) prepurchase exams I've been involved with.

- **Write a job description.** Before you schedule a prepurchase exam, outline your use for the horse so the vet can perform the exam with that in mind. (See, Chapter 2: "Meet Your Match," page 7.) For instance, are you looking for pasture-sound breeding stock, a low-impact trail horse, or a high-level performance horse? Such input is critical for the vet to know.

- **Select the right vet.** Choose a veterinarian you feel comfortable talking to. (For more advice on choosing the right vet, see "Choosing the right prepurchase veterinarian," on page 127.) I look for a vet whose expertise is in my chosen field (performance horses), and who treats the prepurchase as though buying the horse for him- or herself.

- **Go digital.** I recommend a veterinarian who has digital x-ray technology, for the reasons Dr. Heite outlined in the "Choosing" sidebar. (And I always x-ray a horse's front feet and hocks, as this is where you can commonly find problems that can affect performance.)

- **Opt for experience.** Choose a vet who does a LOT of prepurchase exams. Dr. Heite does hundreds a year. A vet who does only a handful may lack the confidence (and knowledge) to offer an opinion.

- **Listen to the vet.** Pinching pennies now won't save you in the long run. Choose a vet you trust, and give him or her a free hand. If the vet recommends a test, do it. It may save you money in the long run.

- **Ask questions.** When you get the vet's input, make sure you understand it. The only stupid question is one you don't ask. Then take the time to discuss it with him or her, your trainer or agent, etc. Make sure you all feel comfortable. If you don't, your guts are telling you something.

- **Use logic.** Take the emotion out of it. This is especially hard when buying a horse for your kid (and if your kid is there). Let the facts—and logic—drive your decision, not your feelings. (And perhaps leave your child at home.)

- **Don't expect a crystal ball.** Don't expect the vet to say what'll happen in two days, much less two years. He or she can only identify what can be seen on that given day.

- **Be prepared to walk.** If you think a horse has been misrepresented, don't waste your money vetting it. Walk away.

- **The ultimate answer is up to you.** Don't expect a "yes" or "no" from your vet. That's why you need to ask lots (and lots) of questions.

- **Face:** Asymmetry, such as a paralyzed or droopy eyelid or lip on one side, could indicate a neurological problem.
- **Hair coat:** A horse's coat says lots about his health. Is his hair healthy and shiny looking? Or dull and unhealthy? Does he have any skin problems, such as a **sarcoid**?
- **Feet/shoes:** I'll note whether his hooves are healthy and well-tended, or chipped, poorly shod, or with **long-toe/low-heel** conformation.
- **Miscellaneous:** I'll make note of any obvious flaws, such as an old **bowed tendon,** that I may want to check in more detail later in the exam.

3. Cardiovascular system. Using a stethoscope, I'll listen to the horse's heart on the right and left sides of his chest to check for abnormal rhythms and **murmurs**. I'll then record the heart rate in two different instances, to check for basic function:
- **At rest (before exercise):** I'll take his pulse, checking for beats per minute within a normal range.
- **After exercise:** How quickly the horse recovers after being briefly longed or ridden will provide insights into his cardiovascular health and fitness.

4. Respiratory system. At the same time I check his heart rate, I'll check his nose for any abnormal discharge, then check his respiration, listening for any abnormal sounds (such as **roaring**) that could indicate a problem.
- **At rest (before exercise):** I'll count breaths per minute, to see if they fall within a normal range.
- **After exercise:** I'll record the breaths per minute again, checking once more for the horse's recovery rate, and listening for any abnormalities, which can become apparent with exercise.

5. Optic system. I'll examine the eyes to check for a problem that could impair vision, such as **cataracts** or signs of chronic inflammatory conditions such as **equine recurrent uveitis**. (If I detect blindness in one eye, the buyer could end the exam there. Some show and event associations forbid a horse with a blind eye from competing.)

6. Gastrointestinal system. I'll listen to the horse's gut sounds, and note any abnormalities. I'll also palpate the midline of his belly to feel for **colic-surgery** scars.

7. Urogenital/reproductive system. If the horse is a stallion or gelding, I'll palpate the scrotal area to check for abnormalities. In a mare, I'll check her external genitalia. (If the prospective buyer is interested in breeding her at some point, I'll perform a basic rectal palpation to check her ovaries and uterine tone, but may refer him or her to a breeding expert for an in-depth breeding exam.)

Don't expect the vet to say what'll happen
in two days, much less two years. He or she can only
identify what can be seen on that given day.

8. Musculoskeletal system. Next, I'll move onto a more detailed exam of the horse's body, legs, and feet.

■ **Body:** I'll run my hands all over the horse's body, from head to tail, feeling for lumps and bumps that could indicate old injuries. (If he's a gray horse, I'll check for **melanomas** under the tail and around his rectum.) I'll also palpate his back, loin, and croup for signs of muscle soreness, which could be due to injury, poor saddle fit, or be a clue to a problem elsewhere, such as in his hocks.

For each leg and foot, I'll perform the following:

■ **Palpation:** I'll examine the leg (and each joint) thoroughly with my hands (and eyes), feeling for any heat, swelling, lumps, or bumps that could indicate a problem, and/or could warrant additional tests, such as ultrasound or radiographs.

■ **Flexion test:** I'll flex each limb such that pressure is exerted on all the joints separately, from the knee/hock down, then hold it like that for 45 seconds (front leg) or a minute-and-a-half (hind leg). When the time's up I'll ask an assistant or handler to immediately trot off the horse. A problem joint that's flexed may show significant pain when trotted.

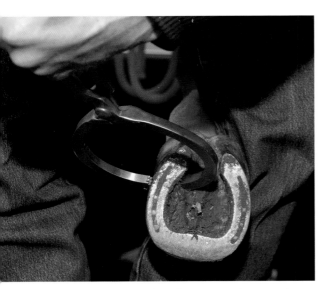

Hoof testers can pinpoint unsoundness and
may tell me if more in-depth testing is needed.

Responses are graded on a scale of 1 to 5. The more positive the response, the higher the score—and potentially the more significant the problem. If I see a positive response, I'll try to ascertain whether the problem is in the upper or lower part of the limb. *Note:* A lot of horses, especially those with some age and mileage, will show a positive response on a flexion test. Repeat flexion tests after the horse has been worked can help your vet evaluate whether there's improvement with work, which may indicate a manageable condition. And further diagnostics, such as x-rays, will help determine whether there's a serious problem behind that response, or a manageable one, such as a mild **bone spur or arthritis** in the lower hock joint. (For more information, see page 137.)

■ **Hoof testers.** I'll apply a hoof tester (a specially designed plier-type device) at various points on the sole

While watching the horse move in-hand (and later, under saddle or on a longe line), I'll look for obvious lameness or asymmetry.

of each hoof, to test for pain/sensitivity, such as from **navicular disease**, that could warrant further testing.

9. Soundness of limb. I'll begin by watching the horse move in-hand, to check for any obvious lameness or asymmetry (which could indicate a neurological problem such as **EPM**). I'll then ask to see him longed, or (preferably) ridden, so I can see him bearing weight, and doing the job you'll want him to do.

- **In-hand:** I'll watch the horse being led toward and away from me at the walk to look for any obvious signs of lameness or asymmetry. I'll then perform a basic neurological exam, such as crossing the horse's front limbs (if he leaves them crossed, I'd suspect a problem); pulling (hard) his tail to one side, then the other, as he walks, to test for balance issues; having him walk in tight circles; and backing him up in a serpentine pattern (also for balance issues). I'll note any perceived abnormalities.

- **On the longe line or under saddle:** I'll ask to see the horse jogged on a hard surface, which magnifies lameness. I'll also watch for subtle variations in stride length, at the walk, trot, and lope on a variety of surfaces. (I'll listen again for any sign of breathing abnormalities at the higher speeds.)

10. Additional tests. Based on the findings from my basic exam, I might suggest one or more of the following:

- **X-rays or fluoroscopy:** Known as *radiographs*, x-rays provide an inside look at boney structures. Again, digital radiography is recommended due to its superior diagnostic capability over standard x-rays and fluoroscopy. Fluoroscopy is a hand-held, video x-ray tool that gives you an inside look in real-time, and can provide a 360-degree view of a joint.

For mature performance horses, I recommend getting the hocks, front feet, and stifles x-rayed due to typical age-related changes, regardless of findings on my basic exam. X-rays can reveal problems that don't show up on flexion and hoof-tester exams.

For young performance prospects, I'd recommend even more views, to check for developmental bone diseases (such as **OCD** bone chips and cysts). Cost: about $35 to $50 per view, for digital x-rays.

Dr. Kurt Heite

Dr. Heite is an FEI (International Equestrian Federation)-certified veterinarian. His practice, Equine Sports Medicine, is in Tomball, Texas. There he focuses on lameness issues in performance horses, often traveling around the country to treat clients' horses.

Eight years ago, he and another FEI-certified, Texas-based veterinarian, Alan D. Donnell, DVM, of Pilot Point, teamed up to provide on-site veterinary services at national-level Western events—and brainstormed an idea for a mobile veterinary clinic. Today, they have two Equine Sports Medicine Mobile Clinics: 18-wheeler conversions that contain the latest in performance-horse diagnostic and therapeutic technology. Special side and rear ramps allow equine patients to enter and exit safely.

The units travel around the country to major Quarter Horse, Arabian, Paint Horse, cutting, and reining events, manned by a rotating group of veterinarians consisting of Drs. Heite and Donnell, plus Dr. David Frisbie of Colorado State University, and fellow DVMs Joe Carter and David Dutton.

Along with his travel and his own thriving practice, Dr. Heite enjoys team roping. His wife, Torrie, also competes. In 2002, she won the APHA amateur 2-year-old halter World Championship. The couple has a daughter, Kassidy, who no doubt will leave her own bootprints in the horse world.

- **Ultrasound:** An imaging technique that uses ultrasonic sound waves to form an image of soft-tissue structures. I'll usually only recommend this test if I suspect a tendon or ligament problem, or if the horse has an old **bowed tendon,** or a suspicious scar over a soft-tissue portion of the leg. Cost: about $125 per leg.
- **Endoscopic exam:** A fiberoptic viewing device on a long, flexible tube is inserted up one or both of the horse's nostrils into the upper airway, to look for cysts and other growths, or the laryngeal paralysis that results in **roaring.** Cost: about $85.
- **Bloodwork:** If something in the basic exam indicates a systemic health check is necessary, I'll pull blood and do a blood chemistry panel and CBC (compete blood count) to check for infection, anemia, and muscle, liver, and kidney function, plus other basic health indicators. Cost: about $70 to $100.

Don't expect a "yes" or "no" from your vet. That's why you need to ask lots (and lots) of questions.

- **Drug screen:** This would inform you as to whether or not any medications such as anti-inflammatories (like "bute") or tranquilizers/mood altering drugs (like reserpine, fluphenazine, and dormosedan) have been given to the horse, which could affect his soundness or disposition. (*Note:* In the case of show-legal medications like bute, if the prepurchase exam occurs at a show, the horse may test positive for that medication.) The seller will (hopefully) be open about any medication the horse has been given. Your prepurchase vet can tell you how this might affect his or her exam findings. (*Note:* I think drug screens can be exceptionally valuable when you don't know the horse or the seller. About 80 percent of my prepurchase clients ask for them.) Cost: about $300 to $1,000, depending on how comprehensive your screening is.

The rundown

At the end of the prepurchase exam, I'll sit down with you and explain what I found and what you can expect, maintenance-wise. Big red flags that would argue against a horse in my book would be:

- **A big OCD lesion in a high-motion joint:** (See "Can you live with it?" on page 136.)

- **A horse that's lame in any way** (unless its pure purpose would be for breeding): That's just the wrong way to start out, especially with a performance prospect. It may be something minor (like a hoof abscess), but why should you pay for a lameness exam for the owner? I'd recommend that you let the seller deal with it. You can check the horse again in 30 days ... if you're still interested.

Radiographs—one of several in-depth tests I might suggest—can help reveal age-related changes or developmental bone diseases not readily apparent from an external examination.

- **A horse that won't load or unload** (and that's going to be hauled by you, the prospective buyer): That's why I like to have horses hauled in for a PPE. That way I (and you) can see how they haul. Most horses will have to be hauled at some point, so loading/unloading problems can be a big deal. Heck, you'll have to get the horse home if you buy him! Hauling to a PPE also gives you valuable insights into how a horse behaves in a new environment.

Can you live with it?

Your prepurchase exam uncovered a problem. Now what? Do you walk away from the horse? Or, can you manage it and keep him sound? It depends. What follows is a chart with a rundown of some common conditions I would and would not want to live with. All of these will likely affect resale value; if you're buying a sale prospect, start with one as trouble-free as possible. (*Note:* These are my opinions. You, your vet, and your trainer will have your own, which is why it's important to gather all the health information you can and discuss it before you make a decision to buy any horse.) The chart starts on page 138.

The arthritis factor

Here are some facts about arthritis I've observed in our sports medicine practice:

- **It's likely.** Commonly the purpose of a PPE is not so much to determine IF arthritis is present, but WHERE and to what extent it is.

- **In the lower hock joints ...** Arthritic changes in the lower hock joints (known as the TMT and DIT joints) are almost a "normal abnormality." That's because arthritis is a common condition found to some degree in almost every performance horse. My favorite analogy is this: Tennis players get tennis elbow. Equine athletes get arthritis.

- **Think genetics.** Certain bloodlines may exhibit more radiographic signs of arthritis than others. However some horses never suffer physically/clinically from this condition from a performance aspect.

- **Think manageable (maybe).** Arthritic conditions can be successfully managed in certain joints (such as the lower hock) for long periods of time.

- **Think permanent.** Once your horse has arthritis, it is not going to go away. It becomes a question of how often you may have to address/treat it and whether you want to manage it if and when the need arises.

- **Ask questions.** Arthritis is common enough that every "older" horse (8 years old, and older) will likely have some degree of arthritic change in a joint or joints. The questions then become: How has it been managed in the past? How is it being currently managed? How do I think I can manage it for the future?

- **Location, location, location.** Each case of equine arthritis should be discussed with regard to specific joint location and current use of the horse. Your PPE veterinarian can answer your questions about how it may affect (or not affect) your horse's performance, and what type of ongoing management may be required.

Can you live with it?

Condition	What it is	Cause
Bone chip in a joint	A piece of bone that breaks loose.	Trauma, or developmental bone disease.
Bowed tendon	Strain and/or tear to the cord-like tendons behind the cannon bone.	Trauma; conformation/shoeing problems can contribute to the risk.
Cataracts	Abnormal scarring in the eye lens.	Congenital (present since birth); trauma; uveitis.
Colic surgery	Horse has had past surgery due to colic.	Colic can be due to heavy parasite load; inadequate diet; motility problems; stress; other unknown causes.
EPM	Equine protozoal myeloencephalitis, as evidenced by seller disclosure or via neurological tests during the PPE.	An infection of the central nervous system caused by a protozoal parasite found nationwide.

Points to keep in mind	Buy the horse?	Red flag
It depends on which joint the chip is in, and where it is in the joint; chips in the knee are harder to maintain than those in the front part of a fetlock; if the chip is near the joint's moving parts, it can be more of an issue (although arthroscopic surgery can potentially fix it with minimal trauma and downtime).	Maybe, if: the chip has been there for some time (as evident by x-rays or seller's disclosure); it's NOT causing painful symptoms (such as lameness, positive flexions, heat/swelling); and you accept that it *could* cause problems down the road, as explained by your PPE vet.	A chip that's causing painful symptoms.
They aren't aesthetically pleasing.	Yes, if: the bow is old and set; the horse is currently sound and working at the level you'll be expecting him to; he has good scar tissue around the site (visible via ultrasound).	Any sign of soreness, lameness, or heat related to the site.
Size matters: large cataracts can adversely affect vision. Also, cataracts can indicate a more insidious problem: uveitis (continue chart for more information on this condition).	Yes, if: it's limited to small scars on the cornea (which is common); they're not inflamed or acute (fresh); are the result of trauma (injury); are only a blemish; and shouldn't hinder eyesight in the future.	Inflammation and/or fresh scarring, which could indicate an inflammatory condition.
If the horse is insured, surgery should be indicated in the records.	Careful consideration is required. A detailed history is key for future care needs and insurance purposes—insurance companies frequently won't cover additional colic treatment/surgery within a certain time period following the initial surgery (usually a year or two without another colic episode).	Any colic episode following the surgery; horses that've undergone previous colic surgeries may be prone to repeat bouts of surgical colic or secondary complications (adhesions) from the first surgery.
Clinically affected/infected horses can be prone to recurrences.	I'd only *carefully* consider it if the horse was showing absolutely no signs of the disease, and even then I'd want to review a thorough history. I'd want to know how long ago the horse had been treated (the longer ago, the better), and what method was used to positively diagnose the EPM.	Any signs of lingering neurological problems—not good in a performance horse, and potentially unsafe.

Can you live with it? (continued)

Condition	What it is	Cause
Equine recurrent uveitis	Chronic/periodic inflammatory condition of the eye that can lead to blindness.	Immune mediated; can result from trauma or unknown triggers.
Heart murmur	Blood moving through the heart makes an abnormal sound.	Can be "normal" in large horses with big hearts (due to blood bouncing around) and in physically fit horses. Or, it can indicate a problem, such as a leaky valve.
Hock changes	Bone spur or arthritic changes in hock, as revealed via x-rays.	Wear and tear; conformation; trauma.
Long-toe, low-heel (LTLH)	A medial-lateral balance issue in the hooves, resulting in an overly long toe and underslung heel.	Natural hoof conformation, and/or poor trimming/shoeing.
Melanoma	Slow-growing skin cancer.	Changes in pigment-producing cells, called melanocytes.
Navicular changes	X-rays reveal changes to the navicular bone in your horse's front foot or feet, which can lead to chronic lameness.	Bad shoeing/trimming; conformation; excessive work.

Points to keep in mind	Buy the horse?	Red flag
ERU can be troublesome to treat/control; potentially performance limiting; can cause permanent damage; and can be expensive to manage/treat (some horses have frequent flare-ups). There is no cure.	Due to all the potential downsides, it would require careful consideration.	Any sign of ocular inflammation.
A murmur due to an abnormality can lead to exercise intolerance (and eventual heart failure).	Only if the murmur is determined to be non-pathologic ("normal").	A murmur determined to be caused by a pathology.
It depends on where it's located. (For more info see "The Arthritis Factor," page 137.	Yes, if: the changes are mild; limited to the lower two hock joints (which are low-motion joints); your vet says they can be managed, say, with periodic joint injections of anti-inflammatory drugs; *and* the horse is currently/consistently performing the job you'll want him to do.	Arthritis in the upper hock joint, which is a high-motion joint; trouble here can be career-ending.
Usually occurs in the front hooves, and causes the most problems there.	Maybe, if x-rays determine it's a shoeing problem, rather than due to bad foot conformation.	LTLH coupled with major navicular changes; LTLH can be a contributing factor in navicular problems.
Commonly seen in gray (and bay) horses, under the tail, adjacent to ears, and around genitalia; severity varies by number, location, and age of horse (more common in older horses).	It depends on severity/location. While melanoma can be locally invasive, these are not the malignant tumors they are in humans. They can usually be easily removed if their location interferes with movement/tack.	I'd be wary if there were a lot of tumors present.
I see more and more sound horses with mild-to-moderate radiographic changes, likely because digital x-ray technology makes them more visible. Keep in mind these changes won't go away, so will be present in any resale PPE.	Possibly, if: the change is in only one foot; the horse is sound; he's currently (and consistently) doing the job you'll want him to do; and he's negative to hoof testers. Still, discuss the pros and cons with your vet.	Walk away if this horse just got pulled up from a pasture and hasn't been working. That's a big clue that he's likely been lame—and laid off.

Can you live with it? (continued)

Condition	What it is	Cause
OCD lesion	A bone cyst or portion of dead bone in a joint that can cause lameness/pain.	Developmental problems; trauma.
Ringbone	Bony changes in the high or low pastern area evident as a bump or scar; verified with x-rays.	Conformation, overuse, or injury/trauma.
Roaring	Whistling respiratory noise when horse lopes/canters.	Paralysis of a laryngeal fold, which partially obstructs the airway.
Sarcoid	Dry, flat, or wart-like skin growths.	A tissue-invading virus.
Sidebone	Calcification of collateral cartilages of the pedal bone, found on either side of the foot protruding above the coronary band; verified with x-rays.	Concussion; conformation; poor shoeing.
Splints	Hard, raised bumps along inside foreleg cannon bones, visible with and without x-rays.	Trauma or conformation issues resulting in inflammation and eventual fusion between cannon bone and sliver-like splint bones.

Points to keep in mind	Buy the horse?	Red flag
OCD lesions are most commonly found in the hocks, though with new technology we're getting better at finding them in stifles and fetlocks; they can require surgery.	It depends on the type and location. In theory, small, shallow lesions may be managed without surgery. I'd consider buying only if the horse is older, sound to flexion tests, and soundly and consistently performing his job.	A bigger, deeper lesion; this is a big red flag, especially in a young horse.
This is typically an older-horse disease; it's generally a progressive one (especially if conformation is to blame).	*Only* if he's a young horse (5 or under) with a scar, meaning it's injury—not conformation—related, *and* he's sound and consistently working.	A horse that's 6 or older, and/or that has any associated arthritic changes.
Horses such as reiners, hunters, jumpers, and speed-event horses need a clean airway, both aesthetically (for judged events) and practically speaking.	It depends on the horse's proposed use. For instance, mild roaring for a recreational trail horse would likely be okay. Plus, surgical correction is an option.	Complications can arise from the surgical correction/treatment of this condition. It may be best to have the seller address/treat the condition first, then re-examine following healing.
Locally invasive, but won't spread internally or all over the body. Can be aesthetically displeasing, and/or interfere with tack. Can be troublesome to treat, depending on location and size.	Perhaps, if lesion isn't located near a high-motion area, or other troublesome spot (near the eyes, nose, and sheath).	A sarcoid located in a trouble spot.
Potential for problems depends on the horse's age and the size of the sidebone—when they get big, they can fracture.	Yes, if: The horse is older, sound, in work, and the sidebone isn't huge.	He's young (4 and under), and has a big one.
Usually this is an aesthetic problem (blemish), though fresh splints may result in soreness.	A fused, "cold" splint is almost always a thumbs up.	N/A; splints are very common and usually only cosmetic.

One way to make sure everyone walks away from a sale happy is to get *all* the terms and conditions, and any other specifics, in writing.

CHAPTER 15

Clinching The Deal

Here's a 4-step strategy for finalizing a sale.

"A wise horseman once told me a sale is not a good sale unless both parties benefit. I believe that statement. For a horse sale to be successful, both you and the seller should walk away happy. Use the tips in this chapter, as well as this book, to help make that happen."

Bob's Personal Experience

You've found the horse you want to buy, after careful research and a thorough in-person evaluation. Now what?

Step 1: Negotiate

Start with price: You knew the asking price before you showed up. I price my horses at what I think is fair. I don't like to dicker. At my barn, you pay that price, or you don't. However, if you find a horse that you think is slightly overpriced, feel free to make an offer. (The worst the seller can do is say "no.") Here are some do's and don'ts for doing so:

- **DON'T** be a tire kicker. Avoid talking price unless you're serious about buying the horse.

- **DO** have a limit, and stick to it. If you can't get that specific horse for your limit, keep looking.

- **DO** go back for a second look, to reinforce your impression before making an offer. If you're still not sure, listen to your gut and walk away.

- **DO** use your trainer or agent for decision-making input and negotiating; that's what you're paying him or her for.

> ### Don't be rude. If you insult the seller in any way, you lose bargaining power. Plus, it's just wrong.

- **DO** ask for a trial period, if that would make you more comfortable about buying the horse. (And know that a lot of sellers won't allow them, due to the risk involved.) See "Trial period tips," page 150.)

- **DO** make it a fair offer. If you're not using an agent, be tactful and respectful, gently stating why you think the horse isn't worth as much as the seller is asking. (An example: "He's still a little green. It would probably cost me about $1,500 in training to get him to the point I'd need him to be....")

- **DON'T** say, "Would you take $X,XXX," then, when the seller says "yes," say "Oh...I'll get back to you tomorrow...." When you make an offer, be prepared to back it up.

- **DO** be prepared to hear a counter-offer. It's common for the seller to offer to split the difference between the initial price and your offer.

Be tactful and respectful as you negotiate a horse's price, and don't hesitate to get your trainer's or agent's input. That way you have the best odds of striking a deal favorable to everyone.

- **DON'T** be surprised if the seller *doesn't* bend on price. If he or she lacks a pressing need to sell, and/or thinks the horse is priced fairly, that's his or her right.

- **DO** be prepared to walk away and let the seller ponder your offer. After he or she feeds the horse for a few more weeks, and spends additional dollars advertising him in an attempt to get the original price, your offer may sound more appealing. Thank the seller for his or her time, and leave your contact information, plus the price you've offered. Remind the seller you'll continue shopping, but that you'd like to hear if he or she reconsiders.

- **DON'T** be rude. If you insult the seller in any way, you lose bargaining power. Plus, it's just wrong.

- **DO** state the contingencies of your offer, for instance that it's contingent upon satisfactory results of a prepurchase exam. (And you WILL have a prepurchase done, right? See Chapter 14: "The Prepurchase Exam.")

No handshake deals! You can find Bill of Sale forms on the Internet by googling "equine bill of sale." Modify it as necessary to mirror your exact agreement, then get everyone involved to sign and date it.

The lease option

Some sellers or trainers will lease a horse that's for sale, which is a great way to spend time with the horse and decide if he's what you want. (It's also a less expensive option than buying, if your budget is constrained.)

Lease situations vary. Some stipulate an "in-barn" lease, meaning you have to keep the horse in the owner's barn. Others will allow you to keep the horse elsewhere, but may stipulate an approved situation (such as you'll need to board and ride with an approved trainer).

Most leases will have you assume all board, care, and training expenses, plus insurance. That may be all that's required to lease the horse, or the owner may tack on a percentage of expenses to make it a "for profit" lease. (Profit leases are most common with top show horses.)

Some people even offer a half-lease, in which you get a predetermined number of days with the horse (such as three days a week), in return for paying half his expenses. A predetermined lease period may be outlined, or the lease may go from month to month.

You also may be able to do a "lease to own" agreement, which is like buying the horse on time. Regardless of what kind of deal you hammer out with the owner, as always, get it in writing and have all parties involved sign the document. For sample lease agreements, go to www.equinelegalsolutions.com, or Google "horse lease forms."

- **DO** offer to put a deposit down on the horse, to "hold" him while you have a prepurchase exam done. After all, the horse will be unavailable for others to try while you're having him vetted. If you opt to purchase him after the exam, you can deduct the deposit from the purchase price. If the exam uncovers a deal-breaking problem, the deposit should be refundable. Be sure to discuss this upfront with the seller.

Step 2: Discuss your method of payment

- **Cash**. This is simplest for both parties, and it can be a powerful bargaining tool. When you show up with cash in hand, the seller knows you're serious. That can work in your favor and make an offer look more appealing.

- **Check, money order, or cashier's check**. While "paper" is less appealing than cash, it's still a universal method of payment. If you're unknown to the seller, he or she may ask for a money order or cashier's check, to reduce the risk of getting insufficient funds.

- **Credit card.** Some farms may be set up to accept credit card payments for horses.

Trial period tips

Some sellers will agree to a trial period before you buy a horse. They may require that you keep the horse at their facility, or may allow you to take the horse to yours. Either way, a trial gives you an opportunity to learn more about a horse over a specified period of time. Here's what to expect if your seller allows one:

- A typical trial period is about two weeks.
- Many sellers require a check for the full purchase price, post-dated to the end of the trial period; if you opt to keep the horse, the sellers will cash the check.
- The seller may also require that any contact you have with the horse be under professional supervision, such as an agreed-upon trainer.
- The seller will require you to assume all responsibility for the horse's care and expenses during the trial period.
- He or she may ask you to agree to a specific standard of care for the horse during this time.
- You should ask for the exclusive right to buy the horse during the trial.
- The seller will likely require that you insure the horse for mortality during the trial term to cover any potential loss. The insurance policy will generally be for the purchase price, payable to both you and the seller, at your expense (generally between one and six percent of the purchase price). It'll be up to you and the seller to determine how to split a payment if the horse should die before he's paid for.
- You may also wish to buy major medical on the horse, to cover any accident- or illness-related expenses he might incur while in your care. For any insurance-related questions, deal with an experienced equine agent licensed in your state. Your veterinarian and/or trainer or agent can help you find a good insurance representative.
- Get any and all terms of the trial period in writing—including what will happen if you opt not to buy the horse—then sign it along with the seller. (For a sample of horse-sale forms that include trial period agreements, go to www.equinelegalsolutions.com, or Google "horse sale forms.")

- **PayPal®.** PayPal allows you to send money to anyone who has an email address, and is being used more and more in horse buys. You bring your laptop computer, and pay from your PayPal account using your credit card, debit card, or bank account. (For more information, go to www.paypal.com.)

"I hope the seller doesn't mind us kickin' this one's tires." (Hint: he will.)

- **Buy the horse on time, with interest.** You arrange to pay over time, generally with a down payment followed by agreed-upon terms and interest rate on the unpaid balance. You won't get any bargains if you ask the seller for terms, but it may enable you to buy more horse than you could afford with a cash deal. Be sure, though, to get all terms in writing. See "Step 3," below.

  Also, the seller will likely require that you insure the horse during the sales contract term to cover any potential loss. The insurance policy will generally be for the purchase price, payable to both you and the seller, at your expense (generally between one and six percent of the purchase price). It'll be up to you and the seller to determine how to split a payment if the horse should die before he's paid for.

  You may also wish to buy major medical on the horse, to cover any accident- or illness-related expenses he might incur while in your care. For any insurance-related questions, deal with an experienced equine agent licensed in your state. Your veterinarian and/or trainer or agent can help you find a good insurance representative.

- **Buy the horse on time, with the owners keeping him until he's paid for.** Some sellers will allow you to make payments on a horse, only if they maintain possession until he's paid for. As with buying the horse on terms, they'll likely require you to insure him. (See info on insurance, above.) As with any aspect of the sale, protect yourself by getting the terms in writing.

Step 3: Get everything in writing

Once you and the seller agree to a price and terms, protect yourself by getting a written agreement to back up your verbal one. You can hire an attorney to do it for you. Or use these guidelines. (General horse bills of sale are also available at such sites as www.findforms.com. Google "equine bill of sale" for other sites that offer forms; we've included a sample one on the next page.)

At the minimum, a bill of sale should include the following, plus the buyers' and sellers'

Sample Bill of Sale

This BILL OF SALE is to certify that on the ___ day of _____, 2___, _____ ("Seller") has sold the horse described below and called _____ to _____ ("Buyer") for the consideration of the purchase price of $_____.

(Insert a full description of the horse, by including color, gender, height, markings, tattoos, or other distinguishing characteristics, and registration number(s), or by reference to and attachment of a copy of relevant passport pages or registry papers as an exhibit to the Bill of Sale.)

Buyer and seller mutually agree as follows:

1) Seller warrants that (a) he has full power to sell the horse; (b) title to the horse is free and clear from liens and is unencumbered; and further, (c) he will defend the same against the claim or claims of persons whomsoever.

2) Seller makes no additional express or implicit representations as to the soundness, health, conformation, or fitness for particular purpose of the horse and Buyer accepts the horse "as is." Buyer has had the opportunity to have a prepurchase exam performed by a veterinarian at Buyer's option and expense.

3) The risks and responsibilities of ownership shall transfer to Buyer as of the signing of this Bill of Sale.

4) Transfer of title to the horse shall be conditioned upon, and effective as of the date of, receipt by Seller of funds in the amount of the total purchase price.

5) This Bill of Sale represents the entire agreement between the parties. No other agreements or promises, verbal or implied, are made or included unless specifically stated in writing and signed by both parties.

6) No commissions or other remuneration have been paid in connection with the sale described herein other than to agents listed below.

7) This Bill of Sale, the enforcement and interpretation hereof, and the transactions contemplated herein shall be governed by the law of the State of _____.

Date _____

Signature of SELLER _____ Social security #: _____

Address _____

Phone _____ Date _____

Signature of BUYER _____ Social security #: _____

Address _____

Phone _____

Remuneration or additional commissions paid: _____

Date _____ Date _____

Agent for SELLER _____ Agent for BUYER _____

Address _____ Address _____

Phone _____ Phone _____

***Reprinted with permission from United States Hunter Jumper Association (www.ushja.org).

signatures (any and all of them). An attorney may suggest additional information to be included; if you have any questions, consult one.

- **Buyer and seller**. Include addresses, phone numbers, and Social Security or tax ID numbers. The seller information on the contract should mirror that on the horse's registration papers, if the horse is registered. (Otherwise, the legality of the sale could be questioned.)

- **The horse.** Include name, age, size, color, breed, sex, registration number (if applicable), brands, or tattoos.

- **Inclusions.** Include any Futurity nominations, promised breedings and/or breeding status (for instance, the horse sells bred or with a foal at her side).

- **Sale date.**

- **Price.** List the purchase price. If you're trading a horse or other property as part of the sale, include the specifics.

- **Terms.** Clearly outline your payment terms. If the horse is to be paid in full on the contract date, say so. If you'll be applying a down payment followed by installments, include the timing, interest rate (if applicable), and any penalties for late or failed payment. Also include who will retain legal possession of the horse and any breed or show registration papers until the horse is completely paid for.

- **Warranty.** Many sellers include no warranty (the horse sells "as is"). It's the old "caveat emptor—buyer beware" approach. (That's where your test-ride protocol and a thorough prepurchase exam will help.) However, if the seller has guaranteed something specific, such as breeding soundness, be sure to get it in writing.

- **Liability.** Identify the agreed-upon date you'll take responsibility for the horse's care, his injury or death, or any injuries he causes.

- **Insurance.** Outline any insurance requirements made by the seller here, should you be buying the horse in installments.

Step 4: Go enjoy your horse!

You've done your homework. Now go play with your new horse. Be safe, and have fun—you've earned it!

First impression: Despite not being fit, this colt has presence and is a good mover. For more, see page 156.

Evaluating
Young Prospects

You can learn a lot about an unridden young prospect's potential—and trainability—by spending a few minutes with him in a round pen.

"If you're an experienced horse person shopping for a yearling prospect for any event (or any unbroke horse), how do you gauge ability—and trainability? (If you're inexperienced, PLEASE stick with well-broke horses.) While there will always be question marks with a youngster, you can hedge your bets by spending some time with him in a round pen.

I'll show you how I check out such a prospect, using two barely halter-broke yearlings fresh from the field. As you'll see, their reactions to me will reveal a lot about their minds and athletic ability."

16

Bob's Personal Experience

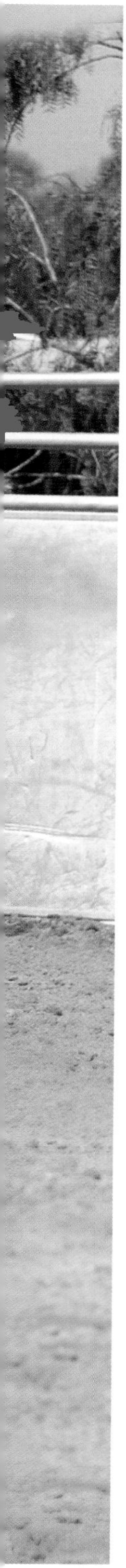

Photos by Darrell Dodds

Thumbs up: He doesn't run through my "barrier."

Good sign: He turns *away* from me, which indicates respect.

A good first impression

1A. As this colt moves freely around the pen (page 154), I can see that he's not fit (he lacks muscling), but he still has lots of presence. He has a pretty head, a good neck that ties high into his chest (which tells me he'll be naturally low-headed), and a pretty shape to his hip. He's also an attractive mover. If his first impression is this positive to me, I know it'll be the same to a judge. So far, so good.

2A. Now I'll push him a bit, by asking him to stop and turn. This will tell me two things: If he has any athletic ability; and if he has a good brain. As I step toward his head and raise my whip to block his path to the right, the youngster immediately rocks back over his hocks (rather than trying to run through my "barrier")…

3A. …and turns into the wall—away from me—planting his weight over his hind end to do so, rather than over his front end. That demonstrates a good degree of natural athletic ability. And, he's showing respect. By turning away from me rather than jumping toward me, he's instinctually not invading my space. That degree of respect, plus the fact he tried so hard to please me, means he likely has a high degree of train-ability.

A cautious, but curious demeanor is another sign of respect—and trainability.

This colt starts out high-headed, and has a weak hind end. Not a great first impression.

4A. I end the session by approaching the colt. His demeanor here reinforces my positive first impression. His eye is kind. He's cautious, but curious, reaching toward my extended hand with his nose, but continuing to respect my space by not walking toward me. He's quiet, almost standoffish, but accepting of my presence. It's another sign of respect. And trainability.

Bad first impression

1B. My first impression of this colt is that he's not one I'd look forward to riding. His neck ties low into his chest, and isn't well shaped. The combination makes him high-headed. In my business, it's hard to win on—or sell—a high-headed horse. His unattractive head makes the image even less flattering. A steep croup and lightly muscled hind end don't improve his profile. (Compare his to the profile of the colt in Photo 1A, and you'll see what I mean.)

Bad sign: He turns *toward* me, rather than away, a sign indicating disrespect.

This colt is not a happy camper. Just look at his pinned ears and pinched face. Would you want to own or eventually ride that kind of attitude? I wouldn't!

His attitude continues as I approach him. He wants no part of me. And I'm more than happy to oblige him by walking away.

2B. When I stepped toward his head and raised my whip to turn him, he ran through my cue the first several times. That's not a good thing. It tells me he disrespects my space, by trampling through it when I use it to block his path. When I finally get him to stop and turn, he jumps toward me—directly into my space. Major disrespect.

3B. Finally, I get him to turn away from me, but he's not happy about it. His pinned ears and pinched expression broadcast his negative attitude, issuing a "trainability alert!" And, he doesn't sit down over his hind end to negotiate the turn, adding an "athletic ability alert!" to the broadcast. Message received.

4B. Just as the seal brown colt reinforced his good impression when I approached him, this youngster seals the deal on a bad impression. His tense ears and expression, coupled with his raised head, tell me he wants no part of me. Like a man ignoring a handshake, he doesn't bother to acknowledge my extended hand. His whole body is saying, "Get away from me." And I'm only happy to oblige.

A great topline like this one equals athletic ability. Read on to see why.

BONUS! CHAPTER 17

Topline Talk

Are you shopping for a top performance prospect? Start by looking at his topline. What does it tell you about a horse's potential? Plenty.

17

Bob's Personal Experience

"Here's how a great topline translates into athletic ability. As you'll see in the photo at left, this reiner has a terrific one. Now look at how it enables him to stop with his head down and his back rounded, so he can break at the withers and loin and really sit down over his hocks. He's doing it on his own, without a rider—because it's natural for him. I'll explain more about what a topline can tell you on the following pages."

Photos by Darrell Dodds

If you're looking for a top performance prospect (or any horse with athletic ability), take a good look at his topline, which is literally the line from his ears to the base of his tail. When it comes to looking at toplines, I have a saying: Head down, back up; head up, back down. That's because how a horse naturally carries his head and neck has a huge impact on his back. And his back has a huge impact on how well he can use his hindquarters…which in turn has a huge impact on his movement and athletic ability.

When a horse carries his neck and head level (or nearly level) with his withers, his back is elevated. That means his entire topline will be nearly level, with no major peaks or valleys. And *that* means he's able to coil up his body, reach deep beneath himself with his hind legs, and propel himself forward in a balanced, athletic—and attractive—frame. That's key whether you're riding cutters or hunters, reiners or Western pleasure horses.

A horse with this type of level topline will be easier to train and ride than one with an inverted topline.

Plus, I personally like the look of "flat-necked" horses, regardless of event. When you're loping circles, these horses give you the look of a bird dog pointing in a field—their topline is beautifully level.

Contrast that with a horse that goes around with his head and neck in the air. When he does, his back hollows. That means he'll drag his hocks out behind his hind end, losing power. To understand how this works, picture a cardboard shoebox, set upside down, with the two long sides cut out so it's resting on the two short sides.

Now imagine the lengthwise surface of the box to be your horse's back, and the short sides to be his legs. Imagine pressing down on his "back," to mimic the hollowing that occurs when he raises his head. Then picture what that will do to his front and hind legs—it pushes them out, away from his body. And that destroys his balance, movement, and athleticism.

In the following photos, I'll help you identify a good topline from a less-good one in two reiners and two pleasure horses. As you'll see, an imperfect topline doesn't mean a horse can't perform, but a good one sure makes it easier for him to do his job—and for you to ride him.

I have a saying: Head down, back up; head up, back down. That's because how a horse naturally carries his head and neck has a huge impact on his back.

The reiners

1. Here's an example of a terrific topline (and living proof of my "head down, back up" theory). This young stallion's neck comes flat out of his wither, which I love. Now look at the distance between his flank and wither—it's short, meaning his back is short. Plus, his back is level, both of which translate into strength. The result? Look how easy it is for him to lift it, so he can reach deep beneath his body with his hind legs, for maximum power—and he's just walking!

This colt rides exactly how he looks, meaning he's easy. When I lope him off, all I do is bring his nose in a bit to keep him soft—he packs his head and neck exactly like this, every time. This horse would have to work at raising them—it wouldn't be comfortable for him.

You saw this reiner stopping in the photo on page 160. Look at his topline in that photo—it's the same as it is here. Sure, he's working in the first photo, rather than walking along, but he's essentially carrying himself the same way, because he's made that way. That means he'll be a lot easier for me to train and ride than a horse on which I'm battling an upside-down build.

A naturally higher-headed horse will have a naturally lower back. Compare this mare's to the colt's on page 162.

2. Compare this mare's back and neck to the stallion's in Photo 1. She's longer in her back (note the distance from flank to wither), and her neck is built to go up, not lie flat. You can see how deeply it ties into her chest, and how it naturally sticks up, out of her wither, rather than emerging level with it. And look what all that does to her back—it hollows it.

I can tell you, she's tough to ride. I'm not saying she can't do anything, but I'm constantly trying to get her to bridle up comfortably. I don't try to get her neck as low as the black colt's, because she's not made to go that way. When I do bridle her up, her neck bows up like a loaded spring. Whenever I release her, it shoots back up in the air, because that's how she's built.

And look at what that does to her legs. Her hollowed back and raised neck cause her to drag her hocks out behind her. That means she has to work harder than the colt does to sit down and stop. She can still stop well, but she sticks her head up high to do it—and she's not as pretty to look at as the black colt is.

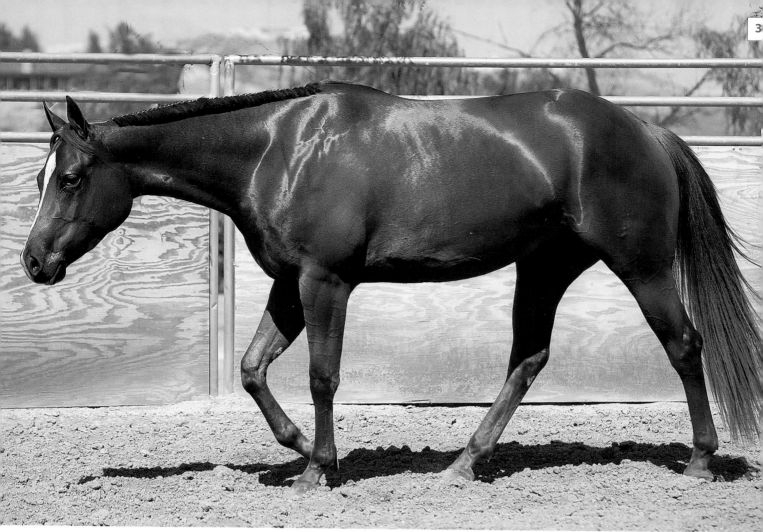

This Western pleasure mare's level topline enables her to easily lift her back and reach deep beneath her body with her hind legs.

An imperfect topline doesn't mean a horse can't perform, but a good one sure makes it easier for him to do his job—and for you to ride him.

The pleasure horses

3. I know this veteran mare well, and I can tell you she goes around with her topline just like this, with a rider and without, all the time. She's built to go that way. She has a long, lovely neck that comes out flat from her withers, and a strong, level back. You can see how that enables her to reach deep beneath her body with her hind legs.

As with many flat-necked horses, she may naturally carry her head a bit lower at the walk and jog (as she's doing here), but when you kick her into the lope (what I call the "money gait"), her topline levels perfectly, which is a sign of balance.

When evaluating young horses at liberty, give them a chance to relax and settle before making a decision.

4. This is my "caveat shot." I put it in to demonstrate that you have to look past circumstances to get a true topline evaluation. This young mare is trotting around with her head in the air. I know her, so I know she's not naturally high-headed. In fact, you can see by the way her neck comes out of her chest (more like the mare's in Photo 3, than that in Photo 2), and how level her back is, that she's built to hold it relatively flat.

This mare was just hauled to a strange place and put in the round pen. Naturally, she's high-headed and "looky" here because everything's new. When evaluating young horses at liberty, give them a chance to relax and settle before making a decision. I have people haul horses over for me to look at, and they expect the horse to be perfect in 5 minutes. That's not going to happen.

When people haul in young prospects for me to evaluate, I'll usually turn the youngsters loose in the round pen for a half-hour, so they can run around and gawk at the new surroundings. Only when a horse looks relaxed will I go back and move him around. That way I get a true read on his potential—not a false impression.

The authors thank trainer Dana Hokana, of Temecula, California, for providing the two pleasure horses used in this chapter.

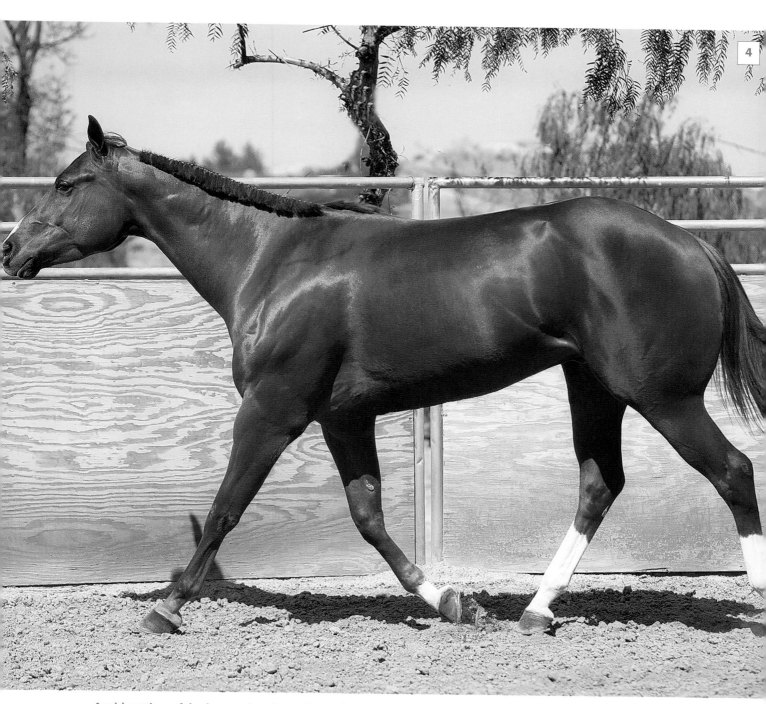

Avoid getting a false impression due to "new place-itis" by allowing a young horse to relax and settle in the round pen before evaluating him. For instance, this mare is not high-headed, as she appears here because she's amped by her new surroundings.

A horse's eyes can be a window to his brain. A big, confident eye like this can mean a confident horse.

The Eyes Have It

Learn what a horse's eyes can reveal about his mind,
so you can up your odds for choosing a good one.

18

"I'm a first-impression guy. When I see a horse, I'll take in his overall look,
then go right to his eye. If I don't like what I see, I'll walk away—and no
one can change my mind about the horse.

Bob's Personal Experience

Photos by Darrell Dodds

Y**ou've likely heard the expression,** "That horse has a good eye." What does it mean? A horse's eyes are the windows to his mind. The ability to recognize a "good" one can help when choosing a prospect.

Here's how to do it:

Good eye

A good eye (at right) usually goes with a good head. This horse is no exception. He has the kind of big, warm eye that I look for. It's alert and has some sparkle, which tells me he's aware of his surroundings without being fearful of them—he radiates confidence.

Such a horse isn't going to zone out on you, which would make him tougher to train than a tuned-in horse. And he's less likely to spook than a less confident, less aware horse.

The lack of white around his eye underscores his confidence and tells me he's probably not spooky by nature. He's not lazy either—I'm not after a dull eye. I want it to be healthy and aware. His starched ears (see page 168) add to his attentive look. If you show, this is the kind of look that'll turn heads in the show pen.

Average eye

Here's an eye that's average in size and appearance (next page, top left). It's a colder, harder eye than that of the previous horse—

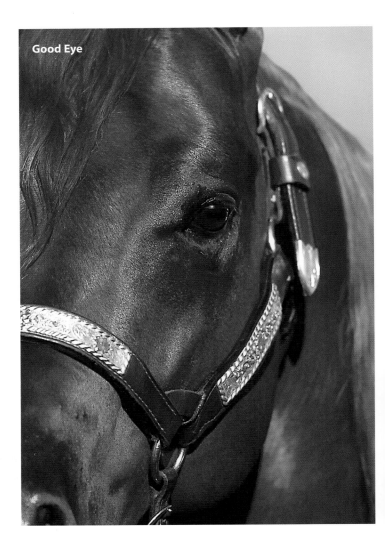

Good Eye

it's simply not as inviting. And the little bit of white around it scares me. Horses with white around their eyes (excluding those for which it's a breed trait) have never been my better ones.

They seem more spooky or quirky than horses without it. Every horse has white around his eyes, you just don't see it until he spooks. The difference is that horses like this one seem to reveal the white even when they're not spooking. To me, that says they're more reactive from the get-go.

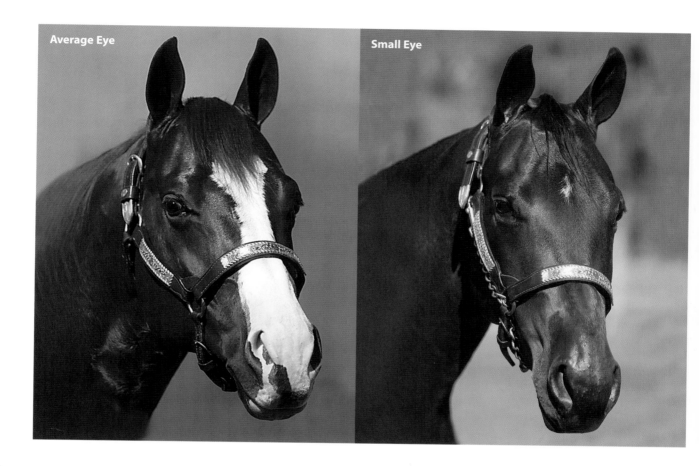

Average Eye

Small Eye

For instance, I know this is a really nice horse who's won a lot. But I also know he can be quirky and reactive. He's different in that way from the good-eyed horse, who's confident and straightforward. I have to work harder on this horse than on that one to get a similar result.

Small eye

To me, a small-eyed horse (above, right) is like a beady-eyed person: I just don't trust 'im. If I were shopping for prospects, I'd probably walk right by this mare. She has a little, hard, glassy eye that detracts from her overall appearance. I happen to know she's not a bad horse—and she's not a great horse.

I find small-eyed horses are the hardest to work with. For instance, this mare does her job, but she doesn't really want to be messed with. And, knowing all three of these horses well, I do trust her the least. So, when shopping, keep an eye on those eyes. They'll tell you a lot!